DISCOVERING THE BIBLICAL Jesus

DANIEL L. AKIN

LifeWay Press®
Nashville, Tennessee

ISBN 0-6330-8761-0

This book is course CG-0957 in the Biblical Studies category
of the Christian Growth Study Plan.

Dewey Decimal Classification Number: 232
Subject Headings: JESUS CHRIST—MESSIAHSHIP \ JESUS CHRIST—PROPHECIES \
CHRISTIANITY—DOCTRINE

Unless otherwise indicated, all New Testament Scripture quotations are from
the Holman Christian Standard Bible®, Copyright © 1999, 2000, 2002, 2003 by Holman
Bible Publishers. Used by permission. Holman Christian Standard Bible®, Holman CSB®,
and HCSB® are federally registered trademarks of Holman Bible Publishers.

Unless otherwise indicated, all Old Testament Scripture quotations and the New Testament
Scripture quotations marked NIV are from the Holy Bible, New International Version,
copyright © 1973, 1978, 1984 by International Bible Society.

Scripture quotations marked NASB are taken from the New American Standard Bible®,
Copyright © 1960, 1962, 1963, 1968, 1971, 1972, 1973, 1975, 1977, 1995
by the Lockman Foundation. Used by permission. (*www.lockman.org*)

Scripture quotations marked NKJV are taken from the New King James Version.
Copyright © 1979, 1980, 1982, Thomas Nelson, Inc., Publishers.

To order additional copies of this resource, write to LifeWay Church Resources
Customer Service; One LifeWay Plaza; Nashville, TN 37234-0013;
fax (615) 251-5933; phone toll free (800) 458-2772;
e-mail *customerservice@lifeway.com;* order online at *www.lifeway.com;*
or visit the LifeWay Christian Store serving you.

Printed in the United States of America

Leadership and Adult Publishing
LifeWay Church Resources
One LifeWay Plaza
Nashville, TN 37234-0175

Contents

About the Author

Daniel L. Akin is the president of Southeastern Baptist Theological Seminary in Wake Forest, North Carolina. Formerly, he was the vice-president for academic administration, the dean of the school of theology, and a professor of Christian preaching at the Southern Baptist Theological Seminary in Louisville, Kentucky. Prior to joining the staff of Southern Seminary, Dr. Akin taught New Testament, theology, and church history at the Criswell College and later was a professor of theology and the dean of students at Southeastern Baptist Theological Seminary. He has pastored a number of churches in Texas, Alabama, Florida, and Virginia. Dr. Akin has led many conferences, including pastors' conferences, Bible-teaching conferences, family-life conferences, and evangelism conferences, and has preached at church revivals.

Dr. Akin holds a bachelor of arts degree in biblical studies from the Criswell College, a master of divinity degree from Southwestern Baptist Theological Seminary, and a doctor of philosophy degree in humanities from the University of Texas at Arlington.

Dr. Akin has written articles for *The Criswell Theological Review, The Southern Baptist Journal of Theology, Evangelical Dictionary of Biblical Theology,* and *Holman Bible Handbook.* He has contributed to the books *Southern Baptist and American Evangelicals, Who Will Be Saved? Defending the Biblical Understanding of God, Salvation, and Evangelism, The New American Commentary,* and *The Holman Bible Commentary.* Dr. Akin has also coauthored two texts for Southern Baptists' Seminary Extension ministry, *How to Understand the Bible* and *Systematic Theology,* and he is the author of *God on Sex,* a popular study of the Song of Solomon.

Preface

Most certainly, the mystery of godliness is great:
[Jesus] was manifested in the flesh, justified in the Spirit,
seen by angels, preached among the Gentiles,
believed on in the world, taken up in glory (1 Tim. 3:16).

Discovering the Biblical Jesus focuses on the central doctrine of Christianity—the person and work of Jesus Christ. From Genesis to Revelation, Jesus is the great theme of the Bible. With bold and beautiful strokes, Scripture paints an incomparable portrait of the Word who "became flesh and took up residence among us" (John 1:14). With false portraits and inaccurate caricatures so prevalent at the beginning of the 21st century, it is imperative that we clearly see and fervently embrace the Bible's teaching about Jesus of Nazareth. What we believe about Jesus, who He is, and what He did will greatly shape the rest of our theology—what we believe about the Bible, God, humanity, the Holy Spirit, salvation, the church, and eschatology (the study of Last Things).

Answering the Jesus question has provoked heated and spirited debate throughout the history of the Christian church. In our postmodern, pluralistic culture, which values a certain form of tolerance above all else, the controversy continues to rage. Exclusive and ultimate truth claims about Jesus Christ do not receive a welcome reception. In this study we will engage the debate head on, looking to God's Word for the right perspective and the right answers to our questions. The Bible, as God's inspired and inerrant Word, is the fundamental way to see Jesus clearly and to understand who He is.

Jesus' coming was promised throughout the Old Testament, and His virgin birth is not mythology but took place in space and time. Jesus is the God-man, complete in His deity and perfect in His humanity. As God's Son, He came into this world to save sinners, and He is the only way to God. We believe this because Jesus said so Himself (see John 14:6). He died on a Roman cross outside the city of Jerusalem and made a perfect sacrifice and atonement for the sins of the whole world (see 1 John 2:2). On the Sunday following His crucifixion, God raised Him from the dead. Jesus' resurrection is not fable or fiction but historical fact. It establishes, by tangible proof, Jesus' lordship over all things (see Phil. 2:9-11; Col. 1:18). Forty days following His resurrection, Jesus ascended back to heaven, where He was exalted at His Father's right hand (see Acts 1:9-11; Heb. 1:3). Jesus' story, however, is not yet complete. The Word of God promises that Jesus will come again to this earth as "KING OF KINGS AND LORD OF LORDS" (Rev. 19:16). This is the "blessed hope" for which Christians wait (Titus 2:13).

In this study we will examine these wonderful truths biblically, theologically, historically, and devotionally. In seeing the biblical Jesus, may we be awed and driven to our knees in gratitude and worship at the magnificence of our Savior. John Knox said, "No one else holds or has held the place in the heart of the world which Jesus holds. Other gods have been as devoutly worshiped; no other man has been so devotedly loved."[1] May God in His grace and goodness use this study to cause us to fall in love with Jesus all over again so that our lives will overflow in gratitude and thanksgiving for Him who loved us so, the One Augustine described as "beauty ever ancient, ever new."[2]

Get the Most from Your Study

Throughout this study you will be asked to complete learning activities. Don't skip them! Take time to write a response to each one. Completing the activities will reinforce your learning and will help you apply what you study.

Before beginning chapter 1, spend a few minutes in prayer asking God to teach you more about Jesus and to lead you to know Him in a more personal way through this study.

Summarize your prayer below. Write directly to God.

_____

_____

_____

_____

_____

_____

Chapter 1
A Savior Is Promised

No person has ever made an impact on the world like Jesus of Nazareth. Whether you embrace Him as your Savior and Lord or reject Him, you can't deny the influence His life has exerted throughout history and around the world. In *Mere Christianity* C. S. Lewis, the insightful Christian apologist, captures something of the impact Jesus made when He came on the scene: "Among these Jews there suddenly turns up a man who goes about talking as if He was God. He claims to forgive sins. He says He has always existed. He says He is coming to judge the world at the end of time. Now let us get this clear. Among Pantheists, like the Indians, anyone might say that he was a part of God, or one with God: there would be nothing very odd about it. But this man, since He was a Jew, could not mean that kind of God. God, in their language, meant the Being outside the world Who had made it and was infinitely different from anything else. And when you have grasped that, you will see that what this man said was, quite simply, the most shocking thing that has ever been uttered by human lips."[1]

Jesus indeed shocked the world. He did things and said things that forced people to make a decision about Him. Once you come face-to-face with this miracle worker and His incredible self-claims, you cannot remain neutral. Some decision, some judgment, must be rendered. Who you think Jesus is becomes an inescapable question demanding an answer. Numerous answers have been offered throughout history, but Lewis helps us narrow the legitimate options that are available.

I am trying here to prevent anyone saying the really foolish thing that people often say about Him: "I'm ready to accept Jesus as a great moral teacher, but I don't accept His claim to be God." That is the one thing we must not say. A man who was merely a man and said the sort of things Jesus said would not be a great moral teacher. He would either be a lunatic—on a level with the man who says he is a poached egg—or else he would be the Devil of Hell. You must make your choice. Either this man was, and is, the Son of God: or else a madman or something worse. You can shut Him up for a fool, you can spit at Him and kill Him as a demon; or you can fall at His feet and call Him Lord and God. But let us not come with any patronizing nonsense

Chapter 1 Learning Goals
- **You will be able to trace the key Old Testament prophecies about the coming of Christ.**
- **Your heart will be filled with gratitude to God for sending His Son to earth to be our Savior.**

Ask God to speak to your heart as you study this chapter.

about His being a great human teacher. He has not left that open to us. He did not intend to.[2]

From this statement derives the famous "trilemma" Lewis posed about who Jesus is—Lord, liar, or lunatic. I would like to add one more possibility: legend. There are four possible answers to the question, Who is Jesus? Let's look at the implications of each one.

Liar—Jesus was not who He said He was, and He knew it. If Jesus of Nazareth was not the Christ, the fulfillment of Old Testament promise and prophecy, the Son of God, and the Savior of the world, and He knew it, He is a liar of the worst sort, and we should scorn Him.

Lunatic—Jesus was not who He thought He was, and He did not know it. If He was not who He thought He was, given His tragically deluded self-understanding, we should pity Him and dismiss Him as a lunatic. This position makes it difficult, however, to explain His remarkable teaching.

Legend—Jesus was not who others later imagined Him to be. If He is just a legend, a make-believe character like Hercules or Santa Claus, we might admire the Gospel accounts for their charm, but we would not view Jesus as the most significant individual to walk the earth, much less worship Him.

Lord—Jesus was who He said He was, and His life, death, and resurrection prove it to be so. If He is Lord; the Son of God; the Messiah; and the risen, ascended, exalted King of kings, we must decide what we will do with Him and how we will respond to this One who is the focus of heaven and earth.

Who Jesus is demands the most serious investigation and consideration. We will start with the Old Testament to learn what it says about the coming of the Messiah, the Savior. Jesus did not appear in a vacuum. He appeared in a historical context. People, especially Jewish people, had hopes and expectations that God would intervene and remove the harsh, oppressive burden of Roman rule. Does the Old Testament help us in our attempt to answer the Jesus question? I believe you will be amazed and encouraged by what a survey of the Old Testament's redemptive narrative reveals.

> Before continuing your study, turn to the front cover and read the title of this study. Now turn to page 3 and read the chapter headings. Briefly state what you might expect to gain from this course.

_____

_____

"From Genesis to Malachi the Old Testament abounds with anticipations of the coming Messiah of Israel."[3]
—*John F. Walvoord*

The First Promise of Redemption: Genesis 3:15

The account of salvation begins in the garden of Eden. In spite of their perfect surroundings, Adam and Eve disobeyed God and plunged all of creation into sin (see Gen. 3; Rom. 8:19-23). Immediately, God took the initiative to remedy the situation, though the cost and loss were (and would be) enormous. In Genesis 3:15 God gave us the first promise of redemption and the first gospel proclamation. Read that verse in the margin.

Addressing the serpent, controlled and used by Satan (see Rom. 16:20), God promised that a male offspring of the woman (Eve) would come and crush the serpent. Someone was coming who would conquer the evil one and restore to humanity what was forfeited when humans disobeyed God in the garden. This Deliverer would come from the seed of woman.[4]

> " 'I will put enmity between you and the woman, and between your offspring and hers; he will crush your head, and you will strike his heel' " (Gen. 3:15).

Read Genesis 3:15 from several translations. Explain in your own words the following statements.

"I will put enmity between you and the woman, and between your offspring and hers."

_____

_____

"He will crush your head." _____

_____

"You will strike his heel." _____

_____

An Everlasting Covenant: Genesis 12:1-3

God promised to send a Deliverer, but where and how would He come? Cain killed Abel (see Gen. 4), and the world became so evil that God had to destroy it with a worldwide flood (see Gen. 6—8). God made a covenant with Noah never to destroy the earth again by flood (see Gen. 9), but then the earth turned away from the Lord at the tower of Babel (see Gen. 11). The whole earth was filled with pride and rebellion. God, however, is faithful

"The Lord had said to
Abram, 'Leave your coun-
try, your people and your
father's household and go
to the land I will show you.
I will make you into
    a great nation
    and I will bless you;
I will make your name
    great,
    and you will be a blessing.
I will bless those who
    bless you,
    and whoever curses you
    I will curse;
and all peoples on earth
    will be blessed through
    you' " (Gen. 12:1-3).

even when we are not. From sinful humanity God called a man and formed a nation through whom He would bless the earth and send His Deliverer. Read God's words to Abram in the margin.

List seven things that God promised Abraham in this passage.

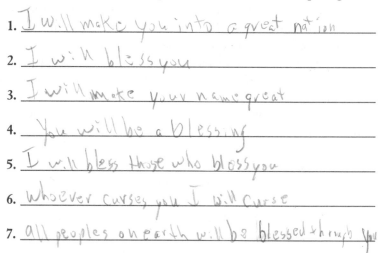

1. I will make you into a great nation
2. I will bless you
3. I will make your name great
4. You will be a blessing
5. I will bless those who bless you
6. Whoever curses you I will curse
7. all peoples on earth will be blessed through you

Abram would give birth to a nation, the nation of Israel. By this man and through his descendants God would bless " 'all peoples on earth.' " Abram, whose name later changed to Abraham, meaning " 'father of many' " (see Gen. 17:5), would be the means by which God would bless the whole world. Allen Ross is right on target when he says, "No one would find divine blessing apart from the blessings given through Abram and his seed."[5] God added to His promise in Genesis 17:7, telling Abraham, " 'I will establish my covenant as an everlasting covenant between me and you and your descendants after you for the generations to come, to be your God and the God of your descendants after you.' "

A Chosen Family: Genesis 49:9-10

Abraham's descendants experienced ups and downs, good times and bad. Yet God kept His word. Through Isaac and Jacob the descendants of Abraham multiplied and settled in Egypt. As he neared death, Jacob gathered his sons and gave what is in essence a prophetic poem (see Gen. 49:2-27) telling them what would be in their future. His words about his son Judah, printed in the margin, are of particular importance because they began to narrow the specific line by which God would bless the whole world.

" 'You are a lion's cub,
    O Judah. ...
The scepter will not
    depart from Judah,
    nor the ruler's staff
    from between his feet,
until he comes to whom
    it belongs
    and the obedience
    of the nations is his' "
(Gen. 49:9-10).

Verse 10 points to the coming of a Deliverer, the Messiah. Allen Ross is again helpful in explaining the significance of this passage:

> This verse moves into the promise for the eschatological [end-time] future, looking beyond the normal period of Israel's history to the dawn of the messianic age. The "scepter" was the symbol of kingship—it would be Judah's. The word is paralleled with "lawgiver's staff" to strengthen the idea that the theocratic administration would remain with Judah. ... God had created humankind to "rule and have dominion" over the earth as his vice regent [see Gen. 1:26-30]. And now, as the plan to restore that blessed estate and purpose for his creation developed, God selected one family with a view to the restoration of rulership. The New Testament affirms that the anticipated King is Jesus the Messiah, the second Adam [see Rom. 5:12-21], a son of David of the tribe of Judah."[6]

A Prophet like Moses: Deuteronomy 18:15

Although Passover (see Ex. 12) and the sacrificial system (see Lev.) hold great significance and symbolism, we are searching for an individual and the picture the Old Testament paints of Him, step by step. He will be born of a woman, an offspring of Abraham and the fulfillment of an everlasting covenant, and he will be a King, a Messiah-King from the tribe of Judah. This is the contribution of Genesis. But let's move ahead to one of the two greatest leaders, alongside David, in the Old Testament: Moses. Moses led the Hebrews out of Egypt; parted the Red Sea; worked miracles; brought the Ten Commandments down from the mountain; and produced the Torah, the first five books of the Old Testament. Given all he had done, the words of Deuteronomy 18:15 are very instructive. Read in the margin what Moses said.

From the greater context (see Deut. 18:15-22) it is clear that God would raise up a series of prophets to follow Moses. Yet Moses said "a prophet like me," and it is interesting to note that in Israel's history the nation began to look and hope for a particular prophet they associated either with or as the Messiah. Thompson points out, "In later times, particularly after the cessation of prophecy, an individual interpretation was given to this passage and 'the prophet who should come' became a figure associated with the Messianic age and sometimes identified with the Messiah Himself (cf. John 1:21,45; 6:14; 7:40; Acts 3:20-22; 7:37, etc.)."[7] God's Deliverer would be someone who would speak for God in an authoritative manner, similar to the way

" 'The Lord your God will raise up for you a prophet like me from among your own brothers. You must listen to him' " (Deut. 18:15).

Moses had. Who He would be, what He would do, and what He would say are continuing to come into sharper focus.

An Eternal Dynasty: 2 Samuel 7

Read 2 Samuel 7. List six promises God made to David in verses 9-16.

Verse 9: *I have been with you where ever you have gone*

Verse 11: *God caused him to rest from all your enemies*

Verses 12-13: *I will set up your seed after you. I will establish the throne of His Kingdom forever*

Verse 14: *I will be His Father and He will be My Son*

Verse 15: *My mercy shall not depart from Him*

Verse 16: *Your throne shall be established forever*

"The Old Testament contains over three hundred references to the Messiah that were fulfilled in Jesus."[8]
—*Josh McDowell*

This chapter records the Lord's great promise to His servant-king David. Other than Moses, no one in the Old Testament is held in higher esteem than this king of Israel, and no one received a more magnificent promise from God. Verses 9-16 identify the specific promises God made to David in what is called the Davidic Covenant:

- " 'I will make your name great, like the names of the greatest men of the earth' " (7:9).
- " '[I will] establish a house [royal dynasty] for you' " (7:11).
- " 'I will raise up your offspring, … and I will establish his kingdom' " (7:12) and " 'the throne of his kingdom forever' " (7:13).
- " 'I will be his father, and he will be my son' " (7:14).
- " 'My love will never be taken away from him' " (7:15).
- " 'Your house and your kingdom will endure forever before me; your throne will be established forever' " (7:16).

God had been working in and through the nation of Israel since the time of Abraham. Now He committed himself to one of Abraham and Judah's descendants in order to fulfill His promises to Adam (see Gen. 3:15), Abraham (see Gen. 12:1-3), and Judah (see Gen. 49:9-10). By means of an unconditional covenant (note the repeated "I wills"), God promised to establish an eternal Davidic dynasty.

This text is a classic example of a prophecy with a dual fulfillment, with both near and far foci. Immediately, David's son Solomon was in view as the one who would continue the Davidic monarchy following David's death. The prophecy also has a distant fulfillment, as verse 16 clearly indicates when it speaks of a throne that will be established forever. This promise now became the focal point of messianic hope and expectation. A future descendant of David would come and reign as Israel's messianic King. Encapsulating the promises made to Abraham and Judah, He would be a blessing to the whole earth and also a sovereign King. Robert Bergen focuses on what this incredible promise entails: "The Lord's words spoken here demonstrate him to be the promise-keeping God; having prophetically placed the scepter in Judah hundreds of years earlier (Gen 49:10), he here secured its place within that tribe. ... David is made the founder of the only royal family the Lord would ever sanction in perpetuity. ... The covenant that the Lord established with the house of David became the nucleus around which the messages of hope proclaimed by Hebrew prophets of later generations were built."[9]

> **"Before the foundation of the world was laid, God, in His divine sovereignty, planned to send His own Son to the cross to be our Savior."[10]**
> —*Anne Graham Lotz*

Read the following passages from your Bible: Isaiah 9:1-7; 11:1-16; 16:5; 55:3; Jeremiah 23:5-6; 30:8; 33:15-26; Ezekiel 34:23-24; 37:24-25; Hosea 3:5; Amos 9:11; Zechariah 12:7-8. All of these passages connect two persons: a person in the past, _David_, with a person in the future, _Jesus Christ_.

So the Deliverer will be a King and a descendant of David. But what kind of King will He be, and in what way will He deal with our sin problem? Let's continue to trace the theme of redemption.

Messianic Promises: The Psalms

The Psalms are some of the most fertile soil in all of Scripture for mining details about God's coming Deliverer. Psalms categorized as royal or messianic include 2; 18; 20; 45; 72; 89; and 110. In addition, the incredible psalm of lament, Psalm 22, is so striking in its similarity to Jesus' crucifixion that many scholars refer to it as the crucifixion psalm. And Psalm 16 promises life beyond the grave. Our journey down God's redemptive road would not be adequate without hearing the beautiful, revealing words of some of these psalms.

Psalm 2. This royal psalm, perhaps composed for the coronation of a Davidic king, calls the king the Lord's "Anointed One" (that is, Messiah; v. 2). Verse 7 is utterly amazing. Listen to what God says about this king:

"You are my Son;
today I have become your Father."

And again in verse 12:

Kiss the Son, lest he be angry
and you be destroyed in your way.

This king is a Son who will rule not just Israel but also the nations (see 2:8-9). All are called to kiss, or submit to, Him. Though Davidic kings in the past could have celebrated their coronation with this psalm, it looks forward to God's eschatological (end-time) King, his Anointed One who will rule over David's house forever. VanGemeren notes that "the second psalm is one of the psalms most quoted in the [New Testament]. ... The first-century church applied the second psalm to the Messiah as an explanation of the crucifixion of Christ by the rulers (Herod and Pontius Pilate), the nations, and Israel (the priests, scribes, and Pharisees). They had conspired together against the Messiah of God (Acts 4:25-28). Paul applied it to Jesus' ministry: his sonship, resurrection, and ascension to glory, which confirmed God's promises in Jesus as *the* Messiah (Acts 13:22-33)."[11] This psalm held hope for a greater day and a greater King all the nations would recognize.

Psalm 16. This prayer song expresses confidence and trust in God in both life and death. Verses 10-11 are crucial for our purpose in their expression of hope beyond the grave. Read those verses in the margin.

This psalm of prayer is also a psalm of prophecy. David is confident in the Lord's provisions, including resurrection, or deliverance from the grave, for God's Holy One. Kidner is correct when he writes, "At its full value ... this language is too strong even for David's hope of his own resurrection."[12] If not David's, then whose?

Psalm 22. When I share the gospel with Jewish persons, I always ask them to consider two texts from their Scriptures: Psalm 22 and Isaiah 53. When you read the words from each, it is as if you were standing at the foot of the cross. Spurgeon called Psalm 22 "the Psalm of the Cross"[13] with good reason. A psalm of lament, it is properly applied first to King David. However, the words of anguish and suffering of the godly Sufferer in the psalm far transcend any experience of David. A righteous Sufferer will be forsaken by God (see vv. 1-2). He will suffer spiritually and physically, experiencing spiritual separation (see vv. 1-2), verbal scorn (see vv. 6-8), personal solitude (see vv. 9-11), bodily suffering (see vv. 12-16), and personal shame (see vv. 17-18). Yet in spite of His great loss, God's Servant rests in the confidence of God's deliv-

"You will not abandon me
to the grave,
nor will you let your
Holy One see decay.
You have made known
to me the path of life;
you will fill me with joy
in your presence,
with eternal pleasures
at your right hand"
(Ps. 16:10-11).

14

erance (see vv. 19-21). He is certain that God will allow Him to proclaim the Lord's name again (see v. 22), even to the ends of the earth (see v. 27).

Kidner well says, "No Christian can read this without being vividly confronted with the crucifixion. It [Psalm 22] is not only a matter of prophecy minutely fulfilled [note in particular 22:1,6-9,14-18], but of the sufferer's humility—there is no plea for vengeance—and his vision of a world-wide ingathering of the Gentiles."[14] This psalm predicts the crucifixion of God's righteous Sufferer one thousand years in advance and several hundred years before the Medes and the Persians would invent this torturous and inhumane method of execution![15] As you read Psalm 22, you would almost think you were reading Matthew 27, Mark 15, Luke 23, or John 19.

> Read Psalm 22 from several translations. Then read Matthew 27, Mark 15, Luke 23, and John 19. Visualize the scenes in your mind. Match the statements from Psalm 22 with the Gospel references.
>
> _d_ 1. "My God, my God, why have you forsaken me?" (v. 1).
> _e_ 2. "All who see me mock me; they hurl insults, shaking their heads" (v. 7).
> _a_ 3. "He trusts in the Lord; let the Lord rescue him. Let him deliver him, since he delights in him" (v. 8).
> _b_ 4. "Dogs have surrounded me; a band of evil men has encircled me, they have pierced my hands and my feet" (v. 16).
> _f_ 5. "People stare and gloat over me" (v. 17).
> _c_ 6. "They divide my garments among them and cast lots for my clothing" (v. 18).
> a. Matthew 27:43; Mark 15:32
> b. Luke 23:32-33; John 19:16-18
> c. Matthew 27:35; Mark 15:24; Luke 23:34; John 19:23-24
> d. Matthew 27:46; Mark 15:34
> e. Matthew 27:39; Mark 15:29; Luke 23:35
> f. John 19:37

Psalm 110. No psalm is more clearly messianic than this king-priest hymn. It bears the marks of a coronation psalm for the Davidic king, but the language transcends any ancient king of Israel. So exalted is the language that the Hebrew people viewed it as speaking of the Messiah even before the Christian era. Paul House notes that "everything promised in Psalm 110 cannot unfold in David's lifetime, so his descendants must be included in some manner."[16] The two verses in the margin particularly call for our attention.

"The Lord says to my Lord:
  'Sit at my right hand
until I make your enemies
  a footstool for your feet.'
The Lord has sworn
  and will not change
  his mind:
'You are a priest forever,
  in the order of
  Melchizedek' "
(Ps. 110:1,4).

Several important observations arise from these two verses.

1. Yahweh (translated Lord) gives to David's Lord authority over all His enemies in words that recall the glory and honor given to God's Anointed in Psalm 2.

2. The verses make this Davidic King a co-regent with Yahweh (see Ps. 89:27).

3. Because of this declaration by the Lord, victory for this Davidic Ruler will extend from Zion against all His enemies (see Ps. 110:2-3).[17]

4. This Davidic Ruler will be a King-Priest but one of a completely unique order. The Lord invokes the oath establishing this King's priesthood. Further, He is to be a Priest forever.

5. His order is not that of Aaron but of the ancient, mysterious king-priest Melchizedek (see Gen. 14:17-20). House says, "A Davidic King will emerge who will rule victoriously as both king and priest, who will defeat all enemies, who will endure forever. Higher privileges could hardly be imagined."[18]

A Coming Deliverer: The Book of Isaiah

Isaiah is the most significant book among the prophecies about the coming of Messiah, the Lord's Deliverer. Texts like Isaiah 7:14; 9:6-7; 11:1-16 and the Servant Songs of 42:1-7; 49:1-6; 50:4-9; 52:13—53:12 are crucial to the developing portrait the Lord paints as redemptive history unfolds. We will briefly examine Isaiah 7:14 and 9:6-7. We will then stay for a while longer in chapter 53 as the picture of a suffering Messiah, a suffering King, begins to emerge.

Isaiah 7:14. Isaiah 7:14, in the margin, was initially a prophecy to King Ahaz (735–715 B.C.) as he faced international threats, but it also had a dual fulfillment with near and far aspects. Ahaz's rejection of the Lord (see vv. 10-12) will bring judgment on him and an apparent end to the Davidic dynasty (see 7:2). However, God will remain faithful to David, as promised in the Immanuel prophecy (meaning *God with us*) of 7:14. In a mysterious and sovereign act a divine-human Messiah will appear.

If Ahaz will not ask for a sign as the Lord had commanded (see v. 12), God will give him one anyway, one with implications for both Ahaz and the future. The virgin will be with child, will give birth to a son, and will call Him Immanuel (see v. 14). This prophecy has a near fulfillment in Isaiah's day. At the time the child's birth was predicted, the woman who was to be the mother would not yet have married or had sexual relations. But the prophecy also had a future, eschatological fulfillment in Jesus.

Although Jewish interpreters did not see Isaiah 7:14 as messianic, Matthew and Luke did. In fact, Matthew quoted this prophecy in reference

" 'The Lord himself will give you a sign: The virgin will be with child and will give birth to a son, and will call him Immanuel' " (Isa. 7:14).

to Jesus (see Matt. 1:23). Further, Isaiah 7:14 connects with Isaiah 9:6-7. God will do something wonderful through Immanuel that the ancient Jewish nation did not fully understand.

Interestingly, this text says the mother herself will name the child Immanuel, for in Him God will uniquely be in the midst of His people. But how can this be? Who can this be? Let's move on to chapter 9.

Isaiah 9:6-7. This wonderful text introduces us to the King with four names. Read these verses in the margin.

Write the four names of the King. *Wonderful Counselor,*

Mighty God, Everlasting God, Prince of Peace

Meditate on ways each name describes how Jesus has made Himself known in your life. List those ways here.

He counsel me through His Word; Looking at the univere

I see how mighty He is; God is eternal; He gives me peace

"To us a child is born,
   to us a son is given,
   and the government will
   be on his shoulders.
And he will be called
   Wonderful Counselor,
   Mighty God,
   Everlasting Father,
   Prince of Peace.
Of the increase of his
   government and peace
   there will be no end.
He will reign on
   David's throne
   and over his kingdom,
establishing and upholding
   it with justice and
   righteousness
   from that time on
   and forever.
The zeal of the Lord
   Almighty
   will accomplish this"
(Isa. 9:6-7).

The passage is also an extension of the virgin conception/Immanuel prophecy of Isaiah 7:14. The year was around 725 B.C. The northern kingdom of Israel (Judah is the southern kingdom) faced an ominous and perilous situation. From the north loomed the threat of Assyria. Tiglath Pileser III had built Assyria into an awesome military machine. Now Shalmaneser V was poised and ready to attack a morally and militarily weakened Israel. In fact, Assyria would attack, sack, overrun, and crush Israel in humiliating defeat in 722 B.C. Families would be fragmented and brutally murdered. The land would be devastated, and economic havoc would be rampant. A proud nation and its people would be brought to its knees in shame and humiliation. The die was cast. The nation's destiny was set (see Isa. 8:21-22).

Yet in the midst of despair and hopelessness a word of hope arrived. The gloom, distress, humiliation, darkness, and death of 9:1-2 would be turned into the rejoicing, joy, light, liberation, and peace of 9:2-5. How? By the coming of the King with four names. E. J. Young paraphrases the hope that would spring from the despair of Israel's immediate circumstances: "There is great rejoicing among God's people, because God has broken the yoke of burden and oppression, and the burden and oppression are removed because the weapons and garments of the warrior are destroyed, and the basic reason for these blessings is that a Child is born. In contrast to the mighty foe of

Assyria and also to the Syro-Ephraimitic coalition, a Child brings deliverance to the people of God."[20]

This child is the same as the child of Isaiah 7:14. There His birth was a sign. Here it is the very means of deliverance and salvation![21] This Davidic Ruler is described in terms that carry messianic hope to an entirely new level. "A child is born" emphasizes His humanity. "A son is given" and "Mighty God" emphasize His what? Dare we conclude that "the expected perfect king will be human and divine"?[22] Government will rest on this child. He will be a King, a Ruler, a sovereign Lord. But look at his titles!

- "Wonderful Counselor" is literally *wonder of a counselor*. This divine Deliverer will be wondrous and unfathomable in His wisdom. With perfect insight and a heart of compassion this One will lead.
- "Mighty God" is always used in the Old Testament to refer to God.[23] This title clearly, directly affirms the Messiah's deity.
- "Everlasting Father" means that the Messiah's fatherhood will last forever. The title *Father* reveals that the Messiah is fatherly now and forever in His compassion, concern, and love for His people.
- "Prince of Peace" indicates that the Messiah will be a King who brings peace. "This one is a Prince, and He seeks the greatness of His kingdom and of Himself not in war, as do ordinary rulers, but in peace."[24] Peace among humans and peace between God and humanity can be accomplished only by One who is Himself God.

Verse 7 is eschatological in focus. This King "will be the final king, the king to end all kings."[25] Of His government and peace there will be no end. He will reign forever as the messianic heir to David's throne (see 2 Sam. 7:12-16).

It is clear that the Messiah will be a great King, a world Savior, and a harbinger of peace. But just how will He accomplish this? What is the means by which His kingdom will be established? Psalm 22 gave us a hint, but who could have imagined that God's Messiah would be a Servant-King? Let's move on to perhaps the greatest passage in all of the Old Testament, perhaps the greatest in all of the Bible.

Isaiah 52:13—53:12. This passage requires our careful consideration. Introducing us to "the suffering servant of the Lord," this text has been called "the most important text of the Old Testament."[26] Delitzsch, an Old Testament scholar, said it "looks as if it had been written beneath the cross upon Golgotha." It is "the most central, the deepest, and the loftiest thing that the Old Testament prophecy, outstripping itself, has ever achieved."[27] The text is the fourth of the great Servant Songs of Isaiah, and it is climactic (see Isa. 42:1-7; 49:1-6; 50:4-9). These five stanzas of three verses each weave the twin themes of exaltation and humiliation into a beautiful tapestry.

> "The whole stream and drift of the Old Testament moves straight to the cross of Christ. The whole New Testament is nothing but the portrait of Christ."[19]
> —*James Stalker*

Spend a few minutes studying Isaiah 52:13—53:12. Beginning with 53:3, list all the things you find in this passage that the Suffering Servant of the Lord will do or things that will happen to Him. Use additional paper as needed.

He is despised & rejected by men | We esteemed Him Stricken Smitten by God and afflicted

A Man of sorrows & acquainted with grief | He was wounded for our transgressions

He was despised | He was bruised for our iniquities

We did not esteem Him | The chastisement for our peace was upon Him

He has borne our griefs and carried our sorrows | By His stripes we are healed

Anyone examining this text confronts a crucial question: who is the Suffering Servant? While many suggestions have been proposed, three main interpretations have eclipsed the rest.

1. Some say the text should be understood corporately. They view this text as either the nation of Israel or the remnant within the nation or as the ideal Israel (see Isa. 49:3). This view developed in medieval Jewish thought, but it fails to explain the work accomplished by the Servant. Israel could not atone for its own sins, much less the sins of the nations.

2. Some say the Servant is Isaiah himself, Hezekiah, Jeremiah, Zerubabbel, or Moses. Yet what is said about the Servant scarcely fits the life or ministry of any of these, nor could Isaiah 53:9b be said of even one of them.

3. Some hold that the Servant is the coming Messiah, the royal Davidic King, the ideal Israelite who is totally committed to and consecrated for Yahweh's will and work. This Servant embodies all that is good in Israel. The picture of the Servant of the Lord, of His mission to Israel and to the world, and of His substitionary suffering is a prophecy of the future.

The New Testament reveals, as does the period of history between the Old and New Testaments, that prior to the cross, Isaiah 53 was not uniformly interpreted or identified with the Messiah. Support for a suffering Messiah from the prophetic literature is found in only two books, Isaiah and Zechariah. Indeed, Jesus' followers rejected the idea of a suffering Messiah, as Peter's perspective in Mark 8:31-34 makes clear.

Yet following the cross and resurrection, an interpretative key was provided that opened the eyes of the early church, and ours as well, to the true identity of the Suffering Servant. In Acts 8:35 Philip the evangelist made

The Lord has laid on Him the iniquity of us all

He was oppressed and He was afflicted

He opened not His mouth

He was led as a lamb to the slaughter and as a sheep before its shearers is silent He opened not His mouth

He was cut off from the land of the living

For the transgression of my people He was stricken

They made His grave with the wicked

It pleased the Lord to bruise Him

His soul was made an offering for sin

The pleasure of the Lord shall prosper in His hand

He shall see the labor of His soul and be satisfied

He shall justify many

He shall bear their iniquities

I will divide Him a portion with the great

He shall divide the spoil with the strong

The Servant is the coming Messiah who is totally committed to and consecrated for Yahweh's will and work.

He poured out His soul unto death

He was numbered with the transgressors

He bore the sins of many

He made intercession for the transgressors

19

"See, my servant will
   act wisely;
   he will be raised and
      lifted up and highly
      exalted.
Just as there were many
   who were appalled
      at him—
   his appearance was
      so disfigured beyond
      that of any man
   and his form marred
      beyond human
      likeness—
so will he sprinkle
   many nations,
   and kings will shut their
      mouths because of him.
For what they were not
   told, they will see,
   and what they have
      not heard, they will
      understand"
(Isa. 52:13-15).

plain to the man from Ethiopia that the Suffering Servant is Jesus, and Isaiah 53 is directly cited no fewer than 7 times in the New Testament and alluded to more than 40 times. In Mark 10:45 Jesus wedded Isaiah's Suffering Servant to Daniel's Son of Man (see Dan. 7:13-14) and thereby redefined for us who and what the Messiah would be.

What does Isaiah 52:13—53:12 tell us that the Servant of the Lord will do? The list is staggering.

- He bore our griefs (see 53:4).
- He carried our sorrows (see 53:4).
- He was wounded for our transgressions (see 53:5).
- He was bruised for our iniquities (see 53:5).
- He was chastised for our peace (see 53:5).
- He healed us by His stripes (see 53:5).
- He bore our iniquities (see 53:6,11).
- He was oppressed and afflicted (see 53:7).
- He was slaughtered (see 53:7).
- He was cut off (see 53:8).
- He was stricken for our transgressions (see 53:8).
- He was bruised by the Lord (see 53:10).
- He was put to grief (see 53:10).
- His soul was made a sin offering (see 53:10).
- He poured out His soul to death (see 53:12).
- He was numbered with the transgressors (see 53:12).
- He bore the sin of many (see 53:12).
- He made intercession for the transgressors (see 53:12).

Formulating an outline of the five stanzas will help us realize the awesome work and suffering of this superlative Servant. Read each passage in the margin as we examine the picture of Him.

The Servant's Exaltation: Isaiah 52:13-15

He is exalted because of His success (see Isa. 52:13). Interestingly, the Lord's Servant never speaks! He "will act wisely" (v. 13)—will accomplish His purpose. He will act so wisely that He will certainly succeed in His mission. He will be "raised," "lifted up," and "highly exalted." The Hebrew words for *raised* and *lifted up* are used in combination four times in Isaiah and no place else in the Old Testament (see Isa. 6:1; 33:10; 57:15). In these other three instances the phrases describe God. God knows and the world should know that the Servant will not fail. He will succeed.

He is exalted because of His suffering (see Isa. 52:14). Exalted in verse 13, the Servant is humiliated in verse 14. Oswalt suggests this translation:

"Who has believed
   our message
   and to whom has
      the arm of the Lord
      been revealed?
He grew up before him
   like a tender shoot,
   and like a root out
      of dry ground.
He had no beauty or
   majesty to attract
   us to him,

"Such a disfigurement! His appearance is hardly human!"[28] People are paralyzed by the horror of His suffering and by the cruelty inflicted on Him.

He is exalted because of His service (see Isa. 52:15). In verse 14 observers are shocked by the Servant's abuse. In verse 15 they are shocked by the Servant's accomplishment. Indeed, they are so surprised that the mightiest on earth—kings—will shut their mouths, an unimaginable thought. Furthermore, what was previously hidden to the Gentile nations will be revealed to them. They had never heard or considered "that it is through the loss of all things that the Savior will conquer all things."[29]

The Servant's Rejection: Isaiah 53:1-3

Isaiah 53:1 naturally flows from 52:15. The people look back and lament and mourn over the fact that they misjudged the Lord's Servant and did not believe the message about Him.

He appeared to be insignificant, not important (see Isa. 53:1). The message about the Servant impressed few. Not many listened.

He appeared to be a nobody, not a somebody (see Isa. 53:2). "Tender shoot," recalling Isaiah 11:1, connects the Servant to the Davidic Messiah. "A root out of dry ground" tells us He was in one sense unimpressive. It appeared that He would not survive. The Servant lacked the regal splendor necessary to attract the nations. His was the stuff of a nobody, not a somebody. This was not what "the arm of the Lord" (v. 1) should look like!

He appeared to be a loser, not a winner (see Isa. 53:3). Despised means *considered worthless.* He was quickly dismissed, rejected as a loser. He was "a man of sorrows," both physical and mental, and "familiar with suffering." What can such a weakling do for us? This is "the arm of the Lord" (v. 1)? We hid our faces from Him: we would not even look on one like Him. "He was despised, and we esteemed him not"—we loathed Him and paid no attention to Him. Surely this man is a loser, not a deliverer.

The Servant's Passion: Isaiah 53:4-6

Verses 4-6 take a dramatic turn, revealing an altogether new perspective. Now we discover why the Servant had pain and sickness. We find out it was all for us. At least 10 times in these three verses the personal pronouns *our, we,* or *us* appear. The suffering of the Servant was not his fault; it was ours.

He bore our sorrows (illness; see Isa. 53:4).

> Surely he took up our infirmities
>   and carried our sorrows,
> yet we considered him stricken by God.

> nothing in his appearance
>   that we should
>   desire him.
> He was despised and
>   rejected by men,
>   a man of sorrows, and
>   familiar with suffering.
> Like one from whom men
>   hide their faces
>   he was despised, and
>   we esteemed him not"
> (Isa. 53:1-3).

> "Surely he took up
>   our infirmities
>   and carried our sorrows,
> yet we considered him
>   stricken by God,
>   smitten by him,
>   and afflicted.
> But he was pierced for
>   our transgressions,
>   he was crushed for
>   our iniquities;
> the punishment that
>   brought us peace
>   was upon him,
>   and by his wounds
>   we are healed.
> We all, like sheep,
>   have gone astray,
>   each of us has turned
>   to his own way;
> and the Lord has laid
>   on him
>   the iniquity of us all"
> (Isa. 53:4-6).

"He was oppressed
    and afflicted,
    yet he did not open
    his mouth;
he was led like a lamb
    to the slaughter,
    and as a sheep before
    her shearers is silent,
    so he did not open
    his mouth.
By oppression and
    judgment he was
    taken away.
    And who can speak
    of his descendants?
For he was cut off from
    the land of the living;
    for the transgression
    of my people he was
    stricken.
He was assigned a grave
    with the wicked,
    and with the rich
    in his death,
though he had done
    no violence,
    nor was any deceit
    in his mouth"
(Isa. 53:7-9).

Smitten by God and *afflicted* indicate that this is the Lord's doing. Many in ancient Israel believed that suffering was the result of someone's sins, and therefore they wrongly assumed that the Servant got what He deserved. The griefs and sorrows He carried were indeed deserved, not by Him but by us.

He bore our suffering (see Isa. 53:5).

> He was pierced for our transgressions,
>   he was crushed for our iniquities;
> the punishment that brought us peace was upon him,
>   and by his wounds we are healed.

The Servant took our disease and gave us health, took our punishment and gave us peace, took our wounds and gave us healing. The Servant suffered in our place.

He bore our sin (see Isa. 53:6). "We all, like sheep, have gone astray." We are prone to get lost, ever unaware of the danger that is about us, oblivious to the consequences of wrong choices. "Each of us has turned to his own way." Each of us has chosen our way over God's way.

> The Lord has laid on him
>   the iniquity of us all.

Since verse 4 we have been immersed in the language of sacrifice and atonement, of substitution and salvation. Examine the words describing our sin: *infirmities, sorrows, transgressions, iniquities, gone astray, his own way.* Meditate on the words of His work: *took up, carried, pierced, crushed, punishment, wounds, laid on Him* (by the Lord!). This language clearly shows that the Servant paid the penalty for our sin.

The Servant's Submission: Isaiah 53:7-9

Here is the exemplary dimension of the Servant's work.

He was submissive in His silence (see Isa. 53:7). "He was led like a lamb to the slaughter and as a sheep … is silent." The theme of the lamb runs from Genesis to Revelation (Isaac, Gen. 22; Passover, Ex. 12; Jesus, John 1:29; Warrior-Lamb, Rev. 5:6). No doubt this verse in Isaiah formed the basis of the declaration by John the Baptist, " 'Here is the Lamb of God, who takes away the sin of the world!' " (John 1:29).

He was submissive in His suffering (see Isa. 53:8). "By oppression and judgment he was taken away." He was given an unfair and unjust trial. His treatment was wrong from beginning to end.

> Who can speak of his descendants?
> For he was cut off from the land of the living.

The Servant of the Lord was executed with no offspring left behind. In that day to die childless meant you were cursed by God, and your life was virtually useless.

"For the transgression of my people he was stricken" (v. 8; also see v. 4). For the transgressions of the people a blow fell on the Servant. That which should have hit us hit Him.

He was submissive in His shame (see Isa. 53:9).

> He was assigned a grave with the wicked,
> and with the rich in his death

is a form of Hebrew parallelism carrying the idea that He was buried among the wicked rich. It should not have ended this way.

> He had done no violence,
> nor was any deceit found in His mouth.

Both by word and deed His life should have turned out different. He died like a criminal but was buried like a prince. Things may not be as they seem.

The Servant's Salvation: Isaiah 53:10-12

The death of the Servant was not a murder or a martyrdom. It was nothing less than a divine appointment!

It was purposed by the Lord (see Isa. 53:10). The Servant was the right person at the right time at the right place following the right plan. "It was the Lord's will to crush him and cause him to suffer." God wanted this to happen. It was no accident. It was His Father who caused him to suffer and [made] his life a guilt offering for sin (see v. 10; see also Lev. 5:1-19). It was God's will that the Servant become an atoning sacrifice for sin. But now we see that His death was not the end. If verse 10b does not teach resurrection, its glorious shadow looms large in the background. The Servant's life and sacrifice were not a waste or a loss, after all. In fact, "he will see his offspring and prolong his days." And best of all, "the will of the Lord will prosper [be accomplished] in his hand." Yes, He was bruised by God, but He was also blessed by God. This was purposed by the Lord.

It was pleasing to the Servant (see Isa. 53:11). Verse 11 should read, "From the anguish of His soul, he will see light and be satisfied by His

> "Yet it was the Lord's will
> to crush him and cause
> him to suffer,
> and though the Lord
> makes his life a guilt
> offering,
> he will see his offspring
> and prolong his days,
> and the will of the Lord
> will prosper in his hand.
> After the suffering of
> his soul,
> he will see the light
> of life and be satisfied;
> by his knowledge my
> righteous servant will
> justify many,
> and he will bear their
> iniquities.
> Therefore I will give him
> a portion among
> the great,
> and he will divide the
> spoils with the strong,
> because he poured out
> his life unto death,
> and was numbered
> with the transgressors.
> For he bore the sin
> of many,
> and made intercession
> for the transgressors"
> (Isa. 53:10-12).

knowledge. My righteous Servant shall justify many, bearing their iniqui-ties." This verse is thematically linked with Jeremiah 23:5-6 and the right-eous Davidic branch, a king who will reign, prosper, and execute judgment and righteousness on the earth. The Servant can rejoice. Though the cost was great, the outcome is still greater. Joy replaces anguish. Light vanquishes darkness. The Servant is satisfied by the knowledge of what has been achieved. And what did He do? He bore their iniquities.

It was provided for many (see Isa. 53:12). The picture in verse 12 is that of a victory parade with the Servant marching out front in the role of con-queror, bringing home the spoils of battle. God will give the Servant those He redeemed, as well as those who rejected Him. Indeed, every knee will bow (see Phil. 2:10-11)! Why does He deserve such honor?

> Because he poured out his life unto death,
>   and was numbered with the transgressors.
> For he bore the sin of many,
>   and made intercession for the transgressors.

Dan Block wonderfully puts it all together: "The messianic hope is a single line that begins in broadest terms with God's promise of victory over the ser-pent through 'the seed of woman' (Genesis 3:15), then is narrowed succes-sively to the seed of Abraham (Genesis 22:18), the tribe of Judah (Genesis 49:10), the stem of Jesse (Isaiah 11:1), the house/dynasty of David (2 Samuel 7) and finally the suffering and slain servant of Yahweh (Isaiah 53)."[31] Rejection was His. Acceptance is ours. The wounding was His. The healing is ours. The stripes were His. The salvation is ours. The price paid was His. The forgiveness is ours. The death was His. But life is ours. What a Servant! What a Savior!

Spend a few minutes in prayer, thanking Jesus for what He did on the cross. Recommit and rededicate your life to Christ.

If you've never trusted Christ as your personal Savior, do so now. Pray a prayer like this one: "Dear God, I know that I'm a sinner, and I'm sorry. I confess to You my sins and my need for salvation. I know that You love me and that Jesus came to earth and suffered on the cross for my sins. I now turn away from my sins and place my faith and trust in Jesus as my Savior and Lord. Thank You for saving me. From this day forward I will live my life for You. Amen." Share your decision with your family, your pastor, and your church.

"Christ ... is the key to the whole Bible."[30]
—W. H. Rogers

The Son of Man: Daniel 7:13-14

Daniel is the most apocalyptic book in the Old Testament because, like Revelation, its New Testament counterpart, it predicts the world's ultimate destiny. Daniel introduces the mysterious Son of Man against the backdrop of judgment against the empires of this world and the victory of God. This is the only overt reference in the Old Testament to the Messiah as the Son of Man. Read this text in the margin.

The language of these verses recalls Genesis 1:28; 2 Samuel 7:12-16; Psalm 2; 8; and Isaiah 9:7. The one described as "like a son of man" has the appearance of a man, but He is much more than a mere mortal. He comes with the clouds, a signature of deity in the ancient world.[32] He is given the rule over all things, coronated by the Ancient of Days—God Himself. He is to be worshiped, and His kingdom is everlasting. This final eschatological Ruler is not just a man. He is "the heavenly Sovereign incarnate."[33]

That Daniel 7:13-14 speaks of the Messiah is a view that dates back to early Jewish and, of course, Christian interpreters. Rabbinic interpreters and the Talmud saw the One described in these verses as God's Messiah.[34] The initial Hebrew readers would no doubt have been mystified by His human and divine characteristics. How could this be? Who could this be? Would any person appear on the scene of human history and lay claim to such prerogatives? When might this occur? Daniel 9:24-27 answers these questions.

Messiah the Prince: Daniel 9:24-27

These verses, in the margin on page 26, reveal God's plan for Israel and all of humankind. They show us that our God has His hand on history and is intimately involved in directing and guiding human affairs.

Daniel was praying in the verses leading up to the prophecy. His prayer was sparked by his reading of Jeremiah 29:10: "This is what the Lord says: 'When seventy years are completed for Babylon, I will come to you and fulfill my gracious promise to bring you back to this place.' " Israel had been in captivity for 69 years. As a result, Daniel began to fast and pray, and God answered him: "While I was speaking and praying, confessing my sin and the sin of my people Israel and making my request to the Lord my God for his holy hill [which is Jerusalem, as we are told in 9:16]—while I was still in prayer, Gabriel, … came to me" (v. 20). Gabriel, of course, was not a man but an angel. His appearance was that of a man.[35] Gabriel came to help Daniel understand God's ultimate plan for the restoration of Israel. Daniel thought this would concern the immediate restoration, but he got much more.

" 'In my vision at night I looked, and there before me was one like a son of man coming with the clouds of heaven. He approached the Ancient of Days and was led into his presence. He was given authority, glory and sovereign power; all peoples, nations and men of every language worshiped him. His dominion is an everlasting dominion that will not pass away, and his kingdom is one that will never be destroyed' " (Dan. 7:13-14).

" 'Seventy "sevens" are decreed for your people and your holy city to finish transgression, to put an end to sin, to atone for wickedness, to bring in everlasting righteousness, to seal up vision and prophecy and to anoint the most holy.

" 'Know and understand this: From the issuing of the decree to restore and rebuild Jerusalem until the Anointed One, the ruler, comes, there will be seven "sevens," and sixty-two "sevens." It will be rebuilt with streets and a trench, but in times of trouble. After the sixty-two "sevens," the Anointed One will be cut off and will have nothing. The people of the ruler who will come will destroy the city and the sanctuary. The end will come like a flood: War will continue until the end, and desolations have been decreed. He will confirm a covenant with many for one "seven." In the middle of the "seven" he will put an end to sacrifice and offering. And on a wing of the temple, he will set up an abomination that causes desolation, until the end that is decreed is poured out on him' " (Dan. 9:24-27).

Gabriel told Daniel that " 'seventy "sevens" are decreed.' " The word *sevens,* which is the best translation, is a generic word like our English *dozen.* In reference to time, it can be used to speak of days, weeks, or years. The best view is years, considering the context (see Lev. 25:1-7; 2 Chron. 36:21). These are literal, not symbolic, years. *To be decreed,* or *determined,* means *to cut out.* God has cut out 490 years of history in His plan for Israel. Six actions that will take place are named in verse 24. The first three are negative, dealing with the elimination of sin. The second three are positive, dealing with the establishment of righteousness.

1. " 'To finish transgression' " refers to the finishing of sin in general.
2. " 'To put an end to sin' " refers to ending sins specifically.
3. " 'To atone for wickedness' " refers to the covering of sins—atonement.
4. " 'To bring in everlasting righteousness' " refers to establishing the millennial kingdom.
5. " 'To seal up vision and prophecy' " refers to the fulfillment and therefore the end of all prophecy.
6. " 'To anoint the most holy' " refers to the millennial temple described in Ezekiel 40—48.

This is God's overarching plan. Gabriel also revealed important particulars of the plan, which scholars have interpreted in several ways. I will offer the schematic that I believe is the best explanation of this challenging text.

God will provide temporary restoration for Israel and eternal redemption through the Messiah: " 'Know and discern that from the issuing of a decree to restore and rebuild Jerusalem until Messiah the Prince there will be seven weeks and sixty-two weeks' " (v. 25, NASB). Overall, the 490-year plan of verse 24 is broken down twice: the 49 years to rebuild the city and the 483 years (which includes the 49) between the command to rebuild the city and Messiah the Prince. The decree to rebuild can be dated to the time of King Artaxerxes found in Nehemiah 2:1-8. According to our calendars, the date was March 5, 444 B.C.[36]

The arrival of "Messiah the Prince" is when Jesus is presented as the Messiah. This occurred at His triumphal entry into Jerusalem. Harold Hoehner dates this as March 30, A.D. 33.[37] The Jews used a 360-day lunar calendar. Starting at 444 B.C. and going forward 483 years of 360 days each, we get 173,880 days. Going from March 5, 444 B.C., to March 30, A.D. 33, is 173,880 days. God knew the very century, year, month, week, day, hour, minute, and second His plan would be accomplished. Indeed, our God has His hand on history. He planned when His Messiah would come. He also preordained when Jesus would die as the suffering Messiah.

God sent His Messiah, but the nation of Israel and the Romans rejected Him. " 'After the sixty-two weeks [and the previous seven] Messiah shall be cut off, but not for Himself' " (v. 26, NKJV). " 'Not for Himself' " indicates that Messiah's death was selfless and that it was provided for others. Because of the Jews' rejection of their Messiah, God will bring retribution. The Messiah was cut off after the 69 sevens (483 years). The 70th week is set apart from the other 69. There appears to be a gap. We do not know when the 70th seven (still in the future) will commence, but we know what it will be like.

" 'Then he shall confirm a covenant with many for one week' " (v. 27, NKJV). Who is *he*? He refers to the nearest antecedent, " 'the prince who is to come' " (v. 26, NKJV). This fits the description of the little horn of Daniel 7:8, or the one popularly called the Antichrist. This man will come to power in the final seven (the tribulation). He will make a treaty with Israel. Then he will break the treaty in the middle of the week: " 'In the middle of the "seven" he will put an end to sacrifice and offering. And on a wing of the temple he will set up an abomination that causes desolation' " (v. 27).

Jesus cited this prophecy in Matthew 24:15: " 'When you see the abomination that causes desolation, spoken of by the prophet Daniel, standing in the holy place' (let the reader understand), 'then those in Judea must flee to the mountains!' " Christ's prophecy seems to have multiple fulfillments. Historically, Christian Jews fled to the mountains during the destruction of Jerusalem. However, the A.D. 70 destruction of the temple cannot be the ultimate fulfillment of Jesus' prophecy, because He said in Matthew 24:21, " 'At that time there will be great tribulation, the kind that hasn't taken place since the beginning of the world until now, and never will again!' " The A.D. 70 destruction would be only a foretaste of what will come at the close of history. However, God's retribution will not be unending but temporary. Jesus taught in Matthew 24:22: " 'Unless those days were cut short, no one would survive. But because of the elect those days will be cut short.' " They are limited to a total of one week, or seven years.

God has the world in His hands, and He has a plan for that world. God has always had His hand on history, even to the time He would send His Messiah.

From Days of Eternity: Micah 5:2

A day of judgment was on Jerusalem's horizon (see Mic. 5:1). However, a promised Deliverer would appear from the tiny, insignificant town of Bethlehem. He " 'will be ruler over Israel,' " and amazingly, " 'whose origins are from of old, from ancient times' " (v. 2). Is there again, at least by implication, an indication that the Messiah will be divine, that in some genuine sense He is preexistent? He is born a baby in Bethlehem, but has He also existed from eternity?

" 'You, Bethlehem
   Ephrathah,
     though you are small
       among the clans
         of Judah,
out of you will come for me
   one who will be ruler
     over Israel,
       whose origins are from
         of old,
           from ancient times' "
(Mic. 5:2).

"In the Old Testament
we have the preparation
for Christ; in the Gospels,
the manifestation of
Christ; in the Book of
Acts, the proclamation
of Christ; in the Epistles,
the doctrine of Christ;
and, in the Apocalypse,
the consummation of the
purposes of God in Christ."[38]
—*W. H. Rogers*

There is no question that the Old Testament picture of the Messiah is mysterious and complex, and step-by-step God revealed who the Deliverer would be and what He would do. Kaiser is correct when he says, "The [Old Testament] writers did consciously and knowingly write and point to the Messiah as being a special son born in the line of David with the special divine nature that belonged to God alone!"[39] This, then, is what we should look for. And this is what we will find in Jesus of Nazareth, a first-century Jew and God's Messiah-Son.

One learning goal for this chapter is for you to be able to trace the key Old Testament prophecies about the coming of Christ. Look up the Scripture references and match them with their teachings.

h	1. Genesis 3:15	a. Jesus quoted from this passage while on the cross.
c	2. Genesis 12:3	
j	3. Genesis 49:9-10	b. The Messiah is called the Son of Man.
d	4. Deuteronomy 18:15	
f	5. 2 Samuel 7:16	c. God promised to bless the peoples of the world through this person.
a	6. Psalm 22:1	
k	7. Isaiah 7:14	d. The Messiah would be a prophet like Moses.
e	8. Isaiah 52:13—53:12	
b	9. Daniel 7:13-14	e. The Messiah would be a Suffering Servant who would die for our sins.
i	10. Daniel 9:24-27	
g	11. Micah 5:2	f. God told David that his throne would be established forever.

g. The Savior would be born in Bethlehem.

h. The Messiah would crush Satan.

i. God planned the exact time when Jesus would die.

j. The Messiah would be from the tribe of Judah.

k. The Messiah would be born of a virgin.

The second learning goal was that your heart will be filled with gratitude to God for the coming of His Son to earth to be our Savior. If this is true for you, close your study by thanking God for the gift of His Son.

Answers to matching activity on page 15: 1. d, 2. e, 3. a, 4. b, 5. f, 6. c
Answers to matching activity on page 28: 1. h, 2. c, 3. j, 4. d, 5. f, 6. a, 7. k, 8. e, 9. b, 10. i, 11. g

Chapter 2
A Life like No Other

The life of Jesus of Nazareth from beginning to end is a fascinating account. Those who wish to understand the first century and the context from which Christianity was born must examine this man. The New Testament provides testimonies of eyewitnesses and those closely associated with these witnesses to show us who Jesus was, what He said, and what He did in His brief life of approximately 33 years. Luke, for example, though not an eyewitness himself, tells us that he carefully researched the events recorded in his Gospel: "Since many have undertaken to compile a narrative about the events that have been fulfilled among us, just as the original eyewitnesses and servants of the word handed them down to us, it also seemed good to me, having carefully investigated everything from the very first, to write to you in orderly sequence, most honorable Theophilus, so that you may know the certainty of the things about which you have been instructed" (Luke 1:1-4).

In this prologue to his Gospel, Luke noted that many had recorded the events of Jesus' life. Eyewitnesses had been the source of their information, and Luke had carefully investigated everything from the first to be certain about what had been taught. When we read a statement like this, it makes modern skepticism about what can be known about Jesus all the more amazing. For example, Peter Bien, a professor of English at Dartmouth College and the translator of Nikos Kazantzakis's infamous *Last Temptation of Christ*, says, "I don't think we know who Jesus was. The Gospels, which were written for political purposes—to convert people—are after the fact. Fifty years at least. Mary? Well, obviously he had a mother, so it had to be somebody—her name doesn't matter. Then one Gospel writer says he was born in Nazareth, the other says Bethlehem. Joseph might have been a shoemaker, not a carpenter. Some traditions said Jesus had brothers, others said Joseph had no other children. What difference does it make? The Gospel writers were novelists. ... I realize much of what we know about Jesus is novelistic. But I act as if it isn't."[1]

Or consider the even more skeptical and somewhat cynical judgment of deceased atheist Jon Murray, the former president of American Atheists: "There was no such person in the history of the world as Jesus Christ. There was no historical, living, breathing, sentient human being by that name. Ever. [The Bible] is a fictional, nonhistorical narrative. The myth is good for business."[2]

Chapter 2 Learning Goals
• **You will gain a greater understanding of key events in the life of Jesus.**
• **You will start developing a closer walk with Christ.**
Ask God to speak to your heart as you study this chapter.

These types of judgments tell us more about the persons who make them than they tell us about the biblical record. A fair, honest investigation of the Bible reveals eyewitness testimony that fits well into the historical world of the first century. Like Luke, we will start our investigation at the very first and survey the major events in Jesus' life. However, we will save Jesus' death and resurrection for separate chapters.

Jesus' Virgin Birth

The virgin birth is critical to our understanding of the union of Jesus' deity and humanity. In the virgin birth God became man—the Word became flesh—as the Holy Spirit and Mary participated in the event. The fact that this actually happened demonstrates that there is no contradiction in the idea that God can take on human nature. God in His essence is certainly beyond human apprehension, and yet the incarnation through the virgin birth demonstrates that He is not wholly other and unknowable.

Furthermore, because the virgin birth is presented in Scripture and is accepted by orthodox Christianity as a bona fide miracle, it becomes something of a test case of someone's belief in the supernatural. Those who deny the virgin birth deny God's supernatural act of incarnation. Moreover, a denial of the virgin birth also repudiates the clear teaching of Scripture.

Attacks against the virgin birth began early in the second century when the Talmud, a Jewish writing, told the story that Jesus was actually the illegitimate son of a Roman soldier by the name of Pandira.[4] A pagan philosopher named Celsus used this story, concocted by Jews, to attack Christianity. The French infidel Voltaire propagated the same story. Right down to our present age influential scholars like Brunner, Bultmann, Tillich, Ferre, Baillie, and Pannenberg have openly denied the virgin birth.

The fact is, although we bow before the manger and sing Christmas carols, many in the church today deny the method of Christmas—the virgin birth.

The Biblical Witness

Several key texts address Jesus' birth: Genesis 3:15 (a veiled reference); Isaiah 7:14 (also see 9:6-7; 11:1); Matthew 1:18-25; and Luke 1:26-38. Possible allusions include Romans 1:3; 5:12-21; Galatians 4:4; and Philippians 2:6. Mark and John do not report the virgin birth, so our knowledge of it comes from the Gospels of Matthew and Luke. Matthew examines the birth from Joseph's perspective and provides a legal genealogy back to David (see 1:1-17). Luke looks at the event from Mary's perspective and provides a natural genealogy back to Adam in 3:23-38. These accounts are complementary.

> **"The most significant event of the centuries took place in ... a stable. ... The most significant thing happened in a manger. Yes, Mary had a little Lamb that night. And her precious little Lamb was destined for sacrifice. There was a tiny Lamb in Bethlehem who was destined for Golgotha's altar."[3]**
> —*Charles R. Swindoll*

Prayerfully and carefully read Matthew 1:18-25 and Luke 1:26-38.
List all the names or titles for Jesus you can find in these verses.

_____

_____

Use a Bible dictionary to learn the meanings of these names.

Jesus: _____

Christ: _____

Immanuel: _____

How has Jesus recently been Immanuel in your life?

_____

_____

Write the fivefold description of who Jesus is from Luke 1:32-33.

_____

_____

_____

> "After he had considered
> these things, an angel of
> the Lord suddenly appeared
> to him in a dream, saying,
> 'Joseph, son of David, don't
> be afraid to take Mary as
> your wife, because what
> has been conceived in her
> is by the Holy Spirit. She
> will give birth to a son, and
> you are to name Him Jesus,
> because He will save His
> people from their sins' "
> (Matt. 1:20-21).

Both Matthew and Luke emphasize Joseph and Mary's innocence, right-eousness, purity, and devotion to God. Matthew 1:19 refers to Joseph as a "righteous man" and reports his desire not to disgrace Mary when he discovered that she was pregnant. Joseph also obeyed the angel's directions in Matthew 1:20-21. Luke records that Mary was chosen for God's purposes, having " 'found favor with God' " (1:30). Her humble, obedient response reflects her heart: " 'Consider me the Lord's slave. ... May it be done to me according to your word' " (1:38).

Matthew teaches us that Joseph was in no way involved in Jesus' conception, although he had normal marital relations with Mary after Jesus was born (see 1:25). Joseph was responsible for naming the child (see 1:25). These

**"The Holy Spirit will come upon you,
and the power of the Most High will overshadow you.
Therefore the holy child to be born
will be called the Son of God" (Luke 1:35).**

actions fulfilled the prophecy of the virgin birth in Isaiah 7:14 (see Matt. 1:22-23). The name Immanuel, which means *God with us,* is also significant. The main point of the virginal conception is that it is a sign that God would act again in the midst of his people (see Isa. 7:14).

Luke, like Matthew, emphasizes that Mary was a virgin and that the entire complex of events was a surprise to her (see Luke 1:29-30). Luke also emphasizes the divine agency of the Holy Spirit. Matthew does not ignore this point, but Luke gives it greater attention. Luke 1:35 shows that the Holy Spirit was the divine agent in the virginal conception.

Luke also makes several important theological points. Luke 1:33 emphasizes Jesus' eternal reign in fulfillment of the Davidic covenant (see 2 Sam. 7:14-16). Luke 1:37 emphasizes the impossibility of the virgin birth apart from a divine miracle. Verses 43-44 emphasize the miracle of recognition by Elizabeth and John. Luke also draws attention to Jesus as the Son of God, which gives Him both His identity and title.

Luke makes the point that Mary's submissive example illustrates the fact that God favors the righteous. Luke 1:38,48 teach that a fruitful person is someone who submits to God and to the enabling power of the Holy Spirit.

In summary, the account of the virgin birth, or the virginal conception, is prophesied in Isaiah 7:14 and is described in Matthew 1:18-25 and Luke 1:26-38. The biblical record reveals that Jesus Christ was born without a human father, was conceived by the Holy Spirit, and was born of the virgin Mary. Emphasizing both Jesus' humanity and divinity, the virgin birth is vital to our understanding of the incarnation.

> The main point of the virgin conception is that (check one)—
> ❏ with God all things are possible;
> ❏ it is a sign that God is going to act among His people;
> ❏ God honored the purity and devotion of Mary and Joseph;
> ❏ God heard the cries of His people;
> ❏ it is a divine miracle.

Did the Virgin Birth Really Happen?

Some scholars, especially those who reject the supernatural, have dismissed the historical nature of the virgin birth. Some do not believe in the virgin birth because of what they see as historical difficulties associated with the biblical accounts of Matthew and Luke. Wolfhart Pannenburg denies the virgin birth because he contends that it conflicts with Jesus' preexistent divinity. He says that "in its content, the legend of Jesus' virgin birth stands in an irreconcilable contradiction to the Christology of the incarnation of the preexistent Son of God found in [the writings of] Paul and John."[5] However, we have no reason to view the two doctrines as mutually exclusive rather than complementary. Christ's preexistence relates to His divinity, whereas the virgin birth relates to His humanity. At a finite point in time, the second Person of the Trinity assumed humanity and was born as Jesus. Erickson correctly notes that there is "no reason why the preexistence [of God's Son] and virgin birth should be in conflict if one believes that there was a genuine incarnation at the beginning of Jesus' earthly life."[6] For those who affirm the witness of the Bible, the virgin birth is "simply the means by which God brought about the incarnation of his Son."[7]

Others who reject the virgin birth claim that it is cast in a mythological and legendary framework. According to this argument, the idea of the Son of God assuming a human nature in the womb of a virgin too closely parallels ancient myths and legends for anyone to take the Christian account seriously. Critics argue that the story of the virgin birth arose from Greek mythology and its many miraculous birth stories.

A careful reading of the Gospel accounts reveals no Greek mythological origin. Luke's virgin birth account is the most Jewish part of his Gospel.[8] When we examine the stories of ways Zeus fathered Hercules, Perseus, and Alexander and of Apollo's fatherhood to Ion, Asclepius, Pythagoras, Plato, and Augustus, we discover that "all these alleged parallels turn out to be quite different from the New Testament accounts. Almost all the pagan accounts involve a sexual encounter."[9] These myths "are nothing more than stories about fornication between divine and human beings, which is something radically different from the biblical accounts of the virgin birth."[10] Jesus was not the product of sexual intercourse between God and Mary.

In the 1970s John Hick, a liberal theologian, and his colleagues argued that the doctrine of Christ's preexistence and incarnation must be abandoned as genuine realities; however, they serve as symbols of the truth that Jesus' birth was special and that He was God's gift to humanity. For these liberal scholars, "the very possibility of such a conception and birth is excluded as a logical consequence of the elimination of the supernatural from history [for] if miracles cannot happen, then by definition there cannot be a virginal conception."[11]

Not surprisingly, the Jesus Seminar, a group of liberal scholars who have taken it on themselves to decide what Jesus really said and did, voted down the biblical account that Jesus was born of a virgin. Jesus' birth "is just another of the pagan stories of gods and demigods, involving as they do sordid liaisons between Olympian deities and mortal women."[12] To the Jesus Seminar, the virgin birth simply represents "theological fiction."[13]

> "The doctrine of the virgin birth is a reminder that our salvation is supernatural. ... The virgin birth is also a reminder that God's salvation is fully a gift of grace."[14]
> —*Millard J. Erickson*

Liberal scholars ignore the fact that in redemptive history the miraculous accompanies God's actions. Evangelicals affirm that God exists outside the world and periodically intervenes within the natural order through miracles. Those who don't believe the virgin birth are confessing their unbelief in the omnipotent God of the Bible. The virgin birth is one of many miracles recorded in Scripture that reveal God's willingness and power to carry out His purposes in surprising, supernatural ways.

The Church and the Virgin Birth

The early church was unanimous in affirming the virgin birth as history. To the early church, "the virgin birth of Christ was no more unthinkable than the other three ways by which people have come into the world (Adam with neither father nor mother, Eve with no mother, and others with both father and mother)."[15] The church's historic creeds also affirmed the virgin birth. The teaching is found in the Apostles' Creed, which reads, "I believe … in Jesus Christ … who was conceived by the Holy Spirit, born of the virgin Mary." The Nicene Creed of A.D. 325 affirms the virgin birth by stating, "… who, for us men and for our salvation, came down from heaven, and was incarnate by the Holy Spirit of the Virgin Mary, and was made man." The fourth creed of the early church, the Chalcedonian Creed of A.D. 451, also bears witness that Jesus was "born of the Virgin Mary."

The teaching of Christ's virgin birth is indispensable to the biblical doctrines of Christ and salvation. We must not deny this teaching, for rejecting the virgin birth is rejecting the Word of God. The fact that this doctrine is taught by God's inerrant Word settles the question for God's people.

Jesus is a miraculous gift to humanity and the world.

The virgin birth is not an obstacle to faith but a help. Because Jesus was unique, He did not enter the world like any other human. He came as God incarnate, conceived in the womb of a virgin by the power of the Holy Spirit. Jesus is a miraculous gift to humanity and the world, "a gift that comes ultimately from God, but comes through Mary in a way that allows one to say that Jesus' origins are both human and divine."[16]

Jesus' Early Years

Following His birth and the shepherds' visit to the stable (see Luke 2:8-20), Jesus was circumcised and then brought to the temple, where He was honored by the prophecy of a man named Simeon and by the testimony of a woman named Anna (see Luke 2:21-38). Later Jesus was visited by wise men (see Matt. 2:1-12). The exact time is unclear, though it could have been even a year later. We should remember that the wise men came to see him in a house, not a stable (see Matt. 2:11), and that Herod ruthlessly massacred "all the male children in and around Bethlehem who were two years old and under, in keeping with the time he had learned from the wise men" (Matt. 2:16). Joseph, being warned by an angel in a dream, took Mary and Jesus and fled to Egypt before the murder of the baby boys and remained there until it was safe to return (see Matt. 2:13-15). Then they went to Nazareth, where Jesus would spend most of his life (see Matt. 2:19-23; Luke 2:39-40).

The time from Jesus' early childhood to the beginning of His public ministry has rightly been referred to as the silent years. The only record we have of a specific event is the family trip to Jerusalem for the Passover when Jesus was about 12. He was left behind for several days and was eventually found astonishing the teachers at the temple with His knowledge (see Luke 2:41-50). Scripture provides only one particular statement made by Jesus, but what He said is significant. When asked by His mother why He had behaved, in her opinion, in such an irresponsible and insensitive manner, causing His parents great anxiety (see v. 48), Jesus responded, " 'Didn't you know that I must be involved in My Father's interest?' " (v. 49). These are the first words of Jesus recorded in Scripture.

How and when did Jesus know that He was God's Son, God's Christ, the Savior of the world? The question is intriguing because the evidence is scarce. Yet it is not by accident that the Holy Spirit moved Luke to record this event, the only one in all four Gospels that tells us anything about what specifically happened to Jesus during the silent years. Jesus' response to His parents points to the fact that the things of God already mattered supremely to Him. He must be involved in the work of divine things, and therefore what better place for Him to be than the temple?[17]

Still more important is Jesus' phrase "My Father's interest." These words draw attention to the intimate relationship He enjoyed with the Father. Even at the early age of 12, Jesus was already aware of a close, filial relationship with the Father and the fact that He was on earth to do His will. Whether He knew all the details of His future, we cannot say. But clearly, He already knew Himself to have an intimate, personal relationship with the Father, the kind only a Son would know.

Luke provided a snapshot of the silent years in Luke 2:51-52. Jesus sets the example for all children in that He was obedient to His parents (see v. 51). He also grew or "increased" through the years "in wisdom and stature, and in favor with God and with people" (v. 52). Jesus' growth was normal and godly. It was natural and spiritual. What a great balance His parents provided in Jesus' upbringing, carefully crafting His life for the future. We will not hear from Him again, however, until His baptism by John the Baptist.

Even at the early age of 12, Jesus was already aware of a close, filial relationship with the Father.

Jesus' Baptism

Read Matthew 3:1-17; Mark 1:9-11; Luke 3:21-22. Then answer:

Why did John the Baptist baptize people? _____

_____

What did John the Baptist say about One coming after him?

_____

Why did John the Baptist not want to baptize Jesus?

_____

Why was Jesus baptized? _____

What did Jesus see and hear when He came up out of the water?

_____

"Jesus, by means of the Incarnation, came to know all the vicissitudes of life: trials, joys, sufferings, losses, gains, temptations, griefs. He entered into them, understood them, and thus became a pattern for us."[18]
—*James Montgomery Boice*

Jesus' baptism is recorded in all three Synoptic Gospels and is alluded to in John (see Matt. 3:13-17; Mark 1:9-11; Luke 3:21-22; John 1:31-34). Jesus came to John the Baptist, His cousin, who was baptizing in the Jordan River. John was hesitant to baptize Jesus, realizing that Jesus' birth was more significant than his own, that Jesus' knowledge and understanding of Scripture surpassed his own, and that Jesus' life required no repentance or confession of sin. If anyone needed baptizing, John needed to be baptized by Jesus (see Matt. 3:13-14).[19]

Jesus, however, admonished John that his baptizing Jesus would " 'fulfill all righteousness' " (Matt. 3:15). John relented and baptized Him, and a remarkable thing happened. The heavens opened, and the Spirit of God descended on Jesus like a dove. Then a voice from heaven said,

"This is My beloved Son.
I take delight in Him!" (Matt. 3:17).

Several questions immediately capture our attention. Why was Jesus baptized? What does it mean that His baptism fulfilled all righteousness? Why did the Spirit descend on Him? What is the significance of the voice from heaven? We can glean the following theological truths from this event.

Jesus' baptism inaugurated His public ministry. The boy we last saw in the temple was now a man about the age of 30. God had prepared Jesus for the mission for which He came, and the time for that assignment to start had come. His baptism was the occasion that began His public ministry.

Jesus' baptism identified Him with sinful humanity. Jesus came to provide salvation for sinners. He would accomplish this by His perfect sacrifice when He died on the cross. At the very beginning of His ministry, He declared His solidarity with sinners, not as a sinner Himself but as the One who came " 'to seek and to save the lost' " (Luke 19:10).

Jesus' baptism publicly declared His submission to His Father's will. Jesus was the Suffering Servant of the Lord (see Isa. 42; 49—50; 53). "But the Servant's first mark is obeying God: he 'fulfills all righteousness' since he suffers and dies to accomplish redemption in obedience to the will of God. By his baptism Jesus affirms his determination to do his assigned work. ... At this point Jesus must demonstrate his willingness to take on his servant role, entailing his identification with the people."[20]

Jesus' baptism was an occasion for a revelation of the triune God. The Son was immersed in the Jordan River, the Holy Spirit came down on Him, and the Father spoke from heaven. It is interesting to note that in Matthew's Gospel Jesus' earthly ministry came to an end with another revelation of the Trinity in the giving of the Great Commission (see Matt. 28:18-20).

Jesus' baptism was an opportunity for God the Father to honor His Son. God's voice from heaven gave assurance to His Son of His love and pleasure in Him and in what He was about to do.

Jesus' baptism was when the Spirit of God anointed Him for His public ministry. While the Scriptures are abundantly clear in their witness to the full deity of Christ, they are equally clear in their witness to His full humanity. During His incarnate state the Son temporarily laid aside the free exercise of His divine attributes. He lived His life in obedience to the Father and in dependence on the Holy Spirit. The Spirit was on Him as He conducted His ministry and accomplished His work of redemption. As He began His Galilean ministry, He read in the synagogue from Isaiah 61:1-2, " 'The Spirit of the Lord is upon Me' " (Luke 4:18).

Jesus' baptism defined and set the course for the type of Messiah He would be. Matthew 3:17 is especially crucial to this observation. The Father's declaration combined Psalm 2:7 and Isaiah 42:1. Psalm 2 is Davidic and messianic, while Isaiah 42 is the first of the Servant Songs. Thus, the

" 'The Spirit of the Lord
   is upon Me,
because He has anointed
Me to preach good news
   to the poor.
He has sent Me to proclaim
   freedom to the captives
and recovery of sight
   to the blind,
to set free the oppressed,
to proclaim the year of
   the Lord's favor' "
(Luke 4:18-19).

Father's declaration set the course of our Lord's ministry. He was indeed the Messiah, but He would realize His messiahship through suffering service.

Carson summarizes, "At the very beginning of Jesus' public ministry, his Father presented him, in a veiled way, as at once Davidic Messiah, very Son of God, representative of the people, and the Suffering Servant."[22] It is no accident, then, that the same Spirit who had just anointed Him immediately led Him into the wilderness to be tempted. His willingness to be this kind of Messiah, a Suffering Servant-King, was immediately put to the test.

Jesus' Temptation

Read Matthew 4:1-11; Mark 1:12; and Luke 4:1-13. Then mark each statement *T* (true) or *F* (false).

_____ 1. It was not God's will for Jesus to be tempted.

_____ 2. Jesus' temptation was not a real experience.

_____ 3. Satan's purpose was to tempt Jesus to sin.

_____ 4. Satan did not know for certain that Jesus was God's Son.

_____ 5. The temptations represented a challenge to Jesus' confidence in God.

_____ 6. It would not have been wrong for Jesus to turn stones into bread because He was hungry.

_____ 7. Satan tempted Jesus to choose an easy way over God's way.

_____ 8. Satan can quote Scripture.

_____ 9. Jesus withstood temptation by using Scripture.

_____ 10. Jesus could have sinned.

_____ 11. Jesus did not sin.

_____ 12. Jesus' temptation experience enabled Him to help us when we are tempted.

_____ 13. Following the temptations, Satan left Jesus forever.

Check your answers as you read the following paragraphs.

"Jesus can truly sympathize with and intercede for us. He has experienced all that we might undergo. When we are hungry, weary, lonely, he fully understands, for he has gone through it all himself."[21]
—*Millard J. Erickson*

Each Synoptic Gospel records Jesus' temptation, with Matthew and Luke providing the most extensive accounts (see Matt. 4:1-11; Mark 1:12-13; Luke 4:1-13). God divinely intended this testing of Jesus (the Greek verb for *tempted* can also be rendered *tested*). Note that the Spirit led ("drove," Mark 1:12) Jesus into the wilderness. The background is Deuteronomy 8:1-5, from which Jesus quoted in His first response to the devil (see Matt. 4:4). There Moses referred to the Lord's leading the children of Israel in the wilderness for 40 years " 'to humble you and test you, to know what was in your heart, whether you would keep his commandments or not' " (Deut. 8:2, NKJV). Here at the beginning of His ministry our Lord was subjected to a similar test and showed Himself to be the true Israelite who lives " 'on every word that comes from the mouth of God' " (Matt. 4:4).

The accounts of Jesus' temptation also reflect a clear comparison to Adam and Eve in the garden. Adam and Eve failed their test in a perfect environment and plunged the whole world into sin (see Gen. 3). By contrast, Jesus was faithful in the barren wilderness and proved His qualification to be the Savior of the world. Jesus was tested/tempted like Israel and like us so that He can be our "merciful and faithful high priest" (Heb. 2:17) and "able to help those who are tested" (Heb. 2:18; also see 4:15-16).

Jesus' baptism and temptation in the wilderness are intentionally connected. Although the temptation account is often used to teach that Jesus is our model for dealing with temptation, which is certainly true, this is not the central meaning. At Jesus' baptism God the Father declared Him to be His Son and to be the Messiah. However, Jesus would fulfill a Servant-Messiah role that would involve suffering and death. Was He truly submissive to the Father's will for His life? Was He qualified to be this kind of Messiah?

Satan's Offer

As we analyze the text, we must keep in mind several factors that were significant to the readers' mind-set in the first century:
- An underlying analogy between Moses and Jesus
- A striking analogy between the nation of Israel in the wilderness and Jesus
- An analogy between Adam and Jesus
- The crucial linkage of Matthew 3:13-17 and 4:1-11
- The significance of the designation "Son" for Jesus

The central persons in this drama were Jesus and the devil. The name Jesus was used to stress, on one hand, His humanity. The title Son of God corresponds, on the other hand, to His deity.

The devil appeared at the end of Matthew 4:1. His sole purpose was to tempt Jesus to sin. The word *tempted* conveys the idea of a solicitation to evil or sin. In the worldview of first-century Jews this is a believable scenario, for they would recognize the devil as an active, personal agent in continuous conflict with God. The word itself means *accuser* or *slanderer*. Now that Jesus had been designated as God's Son in Matthew 3:17, it is not surprising to find the devil showing up to test whether that claim was true.

The devil engaged Jesus in three simple dialogues. Prior to the devil's appearance Jesus had been fasting for 40 days. His only sustenance would have been water. He was hungry—starving, no doubt (see Luke 4:2)—when

"After He had fasted 40 days and 40 nights, He was hungry. Then the tempter approached Him and said, 'If You are the Son of God, tell these stones to become bread' " (Matt. 4:2-3).

the tempter showed up to begin the contest. The first two challenges directly attacked the declaration by the voice from heaven of Jesus' sonship (see Matt. 3:17). The devil did not intend his words " 'If You are the Son of God' " (Matt. 4:3,6) to challenge Jesus' sonship as much as to cause Him to consider just what it meant. "Since You are the Son of God" captures Satan's assumption. What kind of Son will You be? What kind of Father do You have? The wilderness, no food, no crowd, and a cross at the end of the road? This is what God has for His Son?

John Broadus points out that each temptation represented a challenge to the Son's confidence in His Father:

1. The first was a challenge to *underconfidence:* " 'Tell these stones to become bread' " (Matt. 4:3). You cannot count on Your Father even to meet Your most basic needs for self-preservation. You better take care of things Yourself.
2. The second temptation was a challenge to *overconfidence:* " 'Throw Yourself down' " from " 'the pinnacle of the temple' " (4:5-6). After all, God said He would take care of You. You say You trust Him. Prove it.
3. The third involved a challenge of *other-confidence:* " 'I will give You all [the kingdoms of the world] if You will fall down and worship me' " (4:8-9). You are the Messiah, but Your Father's road is hard. It involves a cross. My way is easy. Just drop to Your knees and honor me, and it is all Yours.[23]

Jesus' Response

Jesus' response in His temptation is instructive:

1. Jesus trusted the leading and the control of the Holy Spirit, even when He led Him into the wilderness.
2. To each temptation Jesus responded with the Word of God. Three times Jesus said, " 'It is written' " (Matt. 4:4,7,10). The implication is that the Word stands written for all time. The Word of God has permanence.
3. Each quotation came from the Book of Deuteronomy against the background of Israel's wandering in the wilderness (see Deut. 8:3; 6:13,16).

The devil challenged Jesus to do certain things that Jesus refused to do: turn stones to bread, jump from the wing of the temple, and bow down and worship him. Jesus was steadfast in His devotion and submission to His Father's purpose and plan for His life, regardless of what that might entail.

The third experience is especially significant in this light. God's Son was challenged to give allegiance to Satan rather than to His Father. Such allegiance, by a simple act of worship, would have granted Jesus, the Messiah, something Old Testament prophecy promised Him: the kingdoms of the world. However, the means by which He would obtain these kingdoms was not to be in the fashion the devil proposed. Jesus' submission to God's pur-

" 'It is written:
Man must not live
   on bread alone,
but on every word that comes
   from the mouth of God' "
(Matt. 4:4).

" 'It is also written: You must not tempt the Lord your God' " (Matt. 4:7).

" 'Go away, Satan! For it is written:
You must worship the Lord
   your God,
and you must serve Him
   only' " (Matt. 4:10).

pose would take Him on a different path, as indicated by His Father's words in Matthew 3:17 and the Old Testament Scriptures revealing who the Messiah would be. Therefore, Jesus refused Satan's offers, Satan left "for a time" (Luke 4:13), and the angels came and served Jesus.

Jesus' victory in temptation proves that He was qualified to be Israel's Messiah. He would be the King who obtained His kingdom by being the Suffering Servant of the Lord (see Isa. 53).

Could Jesus Have Chosen to Sin?

For centuries evangelicals have debated the issue of whether Christ could have sinned in His incarnate state. Regardless of the position taken, it is important to affirm two facts from the outset: (1) Christ was genuinely tempted. (2) Christ did not sin.

Those who hold that Christ could have sinned but did not sin point to texts like Hebrews 4:15: He "has been tested in every way as we are, yet without sin." Scripture consistently testifies that our Lord was sinless (see 2 Cor. 5:21). His human nature was like that of Adam and Eve prior to the fall. Jesus possessed no sin nature and never sinned. Yet He was tempted, and if the temptation was genuine, then Christ had to be able to sin. The strength of this view is that it honors Jesus' genuine humanity, emphasizes His identification with human beings, and assures us that His temptations were as real as ours are. The weakness of this view is that it does not sufficiently consider Christ in His person as God. God cannot sin. Christ's deity and humanity cannot be separated. Jesus is now and forevermore the God-man.

Those holding that Christ could not have chosen to sin believe that His temptations by Satan were genuine but that it was impossible for Christ to sin. The purpose of the temptations was not to determine whether Christ could sin but to demonstrate that He could not sin. The temptations came at a particularly significant time: the beginning of Christ's public ministry. The temptations were designed to show the nation of Israel and the world the qualified Savior they had: the impeccable Son of God. It was not Satan who initiated the temptation but the Holy Spirit (see Matt. 4:1; Mark 1:12). If Christ could have sinned, then the Holy Spirit would have enticed Christ to sin because the Spirit led Him into the wilderness. But James 1:13 tells us that God does not tempt anyone.

Some have argued that Christ's freedom to sin could relate only to His human nature and that His divine nature was obviously incapable of sinning. However, Christ's human and divine natures could not be separated. Although He had two natures, He was one person. If the two natures could have been separated, then He could have sinned in His humanity.

> "As a human being Jesus was really tempted. These temptations were not pretended or feigned; they were not designed merely as lessons for his disciples. They were not, one might say, like shadow-boxing."[24]
> —*James Leo Garrett*

But because the divine nature could not sin, Christ could not have sinned.

Furthermore, in moral decisions Christ could have had only one will: to do the will of His Father. If Christ could have sinned, then His human will would have been stronger than the divine will. In addition, Christ had complete authority over His humanity. For example, no one could have taken His life unless He willingly laid it down (see John 10:18). If Christ had authority over life and death, He certainly had authority over sin.[26]

We must hold on with no compromise to the two facts we began with: (1) Christ was genuinely tempted. (2) Christ did not sin. Second Corinthians 5:21 and Hebrews 4:15 make clear that Jesus was sinless. Given that a Barna survey reports that 42 percent of Americans believe that Jesus sinned while on earth, believers are challenged to offer a clear, biblical picture of our sinless Savior.[27]

> **What did you learn from Jesus' temptation that will help you when you are tempted?**
>
> _____
>
> _____

> **"Not only is Jesus Christ eternal, God, but he is God with us. He isn't a God who is far away, distant, and unconcerned; he's with us where we are, sharing the experiences of our lives."[25]**
> —*Warren W. Wiersbe*

Jesus' Miracles

One form of evidence Scripture presents for Jesus' messiahship and deity is His miraculous works. The Gospels record 35 separate miracles that Christ performed. Matthew mentions 20; Mark, 18; and Luke, 20. John built his Gospel around 7 sign miracles. These, however, are not all of the miracles Jesus performed. Matthew, for instance, alludes to 12 occasions when Jesus performed a number of miraculous works (see 4:23-24; 8:16; 9:35; 10:1; 11:4-5,20-24; 12:15; 14:14,36; 15:30; 19:2; 21:14). Each Gospel writer selected according to his purpose from the large number of miracles the Lord Jesus performed.

For example, in the first 11 chapters of John, sometimes called the book of signs, the apostle focused on 7 particular miracles that witness to Jesus' deity and should cause us to put our faith in Him so that we "may have life in His name" (John 20:31). In fact, in John 20:30 the apostle specifically tells us, "Jesus performed many other signs in the presence of His disciples that are not written in this book." In John 21:25 John wrote, "There are also many other things that Jesus did, which, if they were written one by one, I suppose not even the world itself could contain the books that would be written."

John's 7 signs or miracles include the following.

1. Jesus turned water to wine (see 2:1-11).
2. Jesus healed a nobleman's son (see 4:46-54).
3. Jesus cured a paralytic (see 5:1-16).
4. Jesus fed five thousand men (the only miracle recorded in all four Gospels besides the resurrection; see 6:1-15).
5. Jesus walked on water (see 6:16-21).
6. Jesus healed a blind man (see 9).
7. Jesus raised Lazarus from the dead (see 11:1-44).

Of course, the greatest miracle of all occurred when Jesus bodily rose from the dead (see John 20).

Following are five of Jesus' many miracles. Read the account of each one, identify the miracle, and respond to each question.

Mark 4:35-41 is the miracle of _____

What is one storm in your own life or in the life of someone close to you to which you would like for Christ to bring great calm and peace? You do not need to give a written response.

Mark 5:1-20 is the miracle of _____

Who is someone you have never told what Christ has done for you?

_____

Mark 5:21-34 is the miracle of _____
How can you reach out and touch Jesus today? _____

_____

Mark 10:46-52 is the healing of _____

If Jesus asked you, "What do you want Me to do for you?" what would you ask Him to do?

_____

John 5:1-16 is the miracle of _____

"Jesus' response to suffering people and to 'nobodies' provides a glimpse into the heart of God. God is not the unmoved Absolute, but rather the Loving One who draws near."[28]
—*Philip Yancey*

43

If Jesus asked you, "Do you want to get well?" to what area of your life would He be referring? Think about your response, but do not write it.

Pray about what God revealed to you as you studied these miracles.

"When he forgave sins, he did it knowing he was doing what only God can do."[29]
—*James Montgomery Boice*

No aspect of the faith has come under greater attack than the miracles recorded in the Bible. Skeptics like Benedict Spinoza, David Hume, Immanuel Kant, and Julian Huxley have argued that miracles violate the laws of nature, are contrary to human experience and human reason, and have been discounted by modern natural discoveries.

Belief in the supernatural is at the heart of Christianity. Anyone interested in discovering the biblical Jesus must counter with at least five arguments.

1. It is prejudicial and unreasonable to eliminate the possibility of miracles before looking at the evidence. The evidence should form our conclusions and not the reverse.
2. The fact that every event (or effect) has a cause does not mean that every cause must be a natural cause. It is possible that some events (or effects) have supernatural causes.
3. Because God exists, miracles are possible, even probable.
4. Without faith in God, people cannot see the acts of God. They will always seek another explanation, even in the face of overwhelming evidence.
5. Jesus' life and resurrection from the dead are the greatest evidence of the miraculous. He came to earth and into history so that we could know the God who does the supernatural.

Jesus' Transfiguration

The theological importance of Jesus' transfiguration is often overlooked. It is recorded in each Synoptic Gospel (see Matt. 17:1-13; Mark 9:2-13; Luke 9:28-36). Peter also alluded to the event in 2 Peter 1:16-18.

Read Matthew 17:1-13 and 2 Peter 1:16-18. Pretend that you are Simon Peter and witnessed Jesus' transfiguration. Suppose that a few days later someone asked you, "What do you think God was teaching through that experience?" Write your response below.

_____

_____

Peter, James, and John accompanied Jesus to a high mountain. While they were there, our Lord was "transformed" (Matt. 17:2) or "transfigured" (NIV). Then Moses and Elijah appeared before them.

The root of the word translated *transformed* is *metamorphoo,* which "suggests a change of inmost nature that may be outwardly visible or quite invisible."[30] In this case the change was clearly outward. This outward manifestation of Christ's inward reality allowed the disciples "to glimpse something of his preincarnate glory (John 1:14; 17:5; Phil 2:6-7) and anticipate his coming exaltation (2 Peter 1:16-18; Rev 1:16)."[31] The Father's heavenly declaration in verse 5 recalls our Savior's baptism (see Matt. 3:13-17):

> "This is My beloved Son.
> I take delight in Him.
> Listen to Him!" (Matt. 17:5).

Then Moses and Elijah disappeared from the scene (see Matt. 17:8), with only Jesus remaining.

This event in Jesus' life served several significant purposes.

1. It allowed the disciples to receive a foretaste of Jesus' coming exaltation and kingdom.
2. It revealed the glory and deity of the Son of God. For a brief moment the God who had walked among us incognito allowed His deity to shine forth in splendor and glory.
3. It confirmed Peter's confession in Matthew 16:16: " 'You are the Messiah, the Son of the living God.' "
4. It encouraged the disciples in light of Jesus' prediction of His passion in Matthew 16:21.
5. It served as motivation for the task to which the disciples were called in following Jesus. They must deny themselves, take up their cross, and follow Him. The transfiguration declared, "Look whom you are following!"
6. It fulfilled Matthew 16:28: " 'I assure you: There are some of those standing here who will not taste death until they see the Son of Man coming in His kingdom.' " The transfiguration gave the disciples a vision of that kingdom.
7. It declared the Son's unique, definitive revelation of the Father to the world.
8. It was a witness to the Son's superiority to and fulfillment of the Law (Moses) and the Prophets (Elijah).
9. It reaffirmed the Father's love for and delight in His Son.
10. It restated that Jesus was the Messiah (see Ps. 2) who would realize His kingdom as the Suffering Servant of the Lord (see Isa. 42). Carson is correct when he says, "The narrative is clearly a major turning point in

"He was transformed in front of them, and His face shone like the sun. Even His clothes became as white as the light. Suddenly, Moses and Elijah appeared to them, talking with Him" (Matt. 17:2-3).

Jesus' self-disclosure. … The contrast between what Jesus had just predicted would be his fate ([Matt.] 16:21) and this glorious sight would one day prompt Jesus' disciples to marvel at the self-humiliation that brought him to the cross and to glimpse a little of the height to which he had been raised by his vindicating resurrection and ascension."[32]

We will address the crucifixion in chapter 4, and we will devote chapter 5 to the resurrection. However, no survey of the major events in Christ's life would be complete without a look at that which brought His first advent to a close: His ascension back to heaven.

Jesus' Ascension

Jerry Vines, the pastor of First Baptist Church in Jacksonville, Florida, and a dear friend, preached a sermon that has had such a profound impact on my life that I listened to a tape of it almost weekly for several years. With his permission I will allow his message on the ascension to guide us through this significant event and doctrine.

Carried Up into Heaven

The ascension of our Lord is recorded only in Luke's two-volume work, in Luke 24:50-53 and Acts 1:9-11. Vines notes that this "is a particular aspect of our Lord's ministry which is neglected in many of our books and is very seldom mentioned in our theologies." What is the significance of our Lord's ascension, and what will a careful consideration of it reveal?

The ascension of Jesus Christ marks the conclusion of His earthly ministry and the initiation of His heavenly session. Jesus' incarnation is inseparably linked to significant events in His life like His incarnation, crucifixion, resurrection, and exaltation.

When Jesus ascended, He led His disciples out to Bethany on the slopes of the Mount of Olives. From there He ascended back to heaven. Vines eloquently describes what happened: "Suddenly the strongest law in the universe was broken! That law which keeps the earth in place; that law which causes planets to whirl around the sun; that law, the universal law of gravitation, was relaxed or suspended or broken to let go free the Son of God! That law could hold on to the stars and keep them in their places, but it could not hold on to the Bright and Morning Star! That law of gravitation could keep the sun in place, but it could not keep the Son of righteousness from arising with healing in His wings! Jesus Christ ascended back."

> **"He led them out as far as Bethany, and lifting up His hands He blessed them. And while He was blessing them, He left them and was carried up into heaven. After worshiping Him, they returned to Jerusalem with great joy. And they were continually in the temple complex blessing God"** (Luke 24:50-53).

At God's Right Hand

Ephesians 4:10 says, "The One who descended is the same as the One who ascended far above all the heavens, that He might fill all things." He went above the first heaven, where the birds fly and the clouds are formed; He went above the second heaven, where the Milky Way is and innumerable stars appear; He went into the very heaven of heavens itself, the place of the throne of God! First Peter 3:22 says, "He has gone into heaven, He is at God's right hand, with angels, authorities, and powers subjected to him." Glorified humanity is now in heaven. A man is on the throne in heaven, the God-man Jesus Christ. The Bible teaches that Jesus ascended to heaven for us, for our benefit. In John 16:7 Jesus said, " 'It is for your benefit that I go away, because if I don't go away the Counselor will not come to you. If I go, I will send Him to you.' " And in John 14:12 Jesus said, " 'I assure you: The one who believes in Me … will do even greater works than these, because I am going to the Father.' "

Jesus ascended to heaven as our Master (see Col. 4:1). He now sits at the right hand of the throne of God, where He resides as the Lord of this universe. In Acts 2:33-36 Peter says, "Since He has been exalted to the right hand of God, … God has made this Jesus … both Lord and Messiah.' " Because Jesus is in heaven, He is our ascended Lord; He is the Master, with angels and authorities subject to Him.

Stephen Olford tells the story of an African village where the chief had died, and it was time to elect a new chief. A man named Dazie was campaigning to be the new chief. Some of his opponents had raised questions about his love for the tribe. On the day of the election Dazie stood before his tribesmen and said, "Some of you have doubted my love." He began to recount the story of the day a leopard attacked the village. He reminded them how many lives were taken. Dazie ran to the leopard and thrust his arm into his mouth, crushing the head of the leopard but also mangling his arm. Dazie said to them, "If I didn't love you, I would not have faced death for you." Then he lifted his mangled arm and said, "In the name of my wounds I claim to be your leader!" Luke says that when our Savior ascended, He lifted up His hands as if to say, "Do you see these wounds? These are the tokens of My love. In the name of My wounds I demand the right to be your Lord!"

Jesus ascended to heaven as our forerunner (see Heb. 6:19-20). As our great forerunner, Jesus Christ has gone into the very holy of holies in heaven as our High Priest. Hebrews 10:11-12 reminds us, "Every priest stands day after day ministering and offering time after time the same sacrifices, which can never take away sins. But this man, after offering one sacrifice for sins forever, sat down at the right hand of God."

"We have this hope—like a sure and firm anchor of the soul—that enters the inner sanctuary behind the curtain. Jesus has entered there on our behalf as a forerunner, because He has become a 'high priest forever in the order of Melchizedek' " (Heb. 6:19-20).

Read Hebrews 10:11-12. Why do you think it is significant that Jesus sits at the right hand of God, in contrast to the Old Testament priests who stood?

_____

_____

In His present ministry Jesus "always lives to intercede" for us (see Heb. 7:25). Paul wrote that Jesus "is at the right hand of God and intercedes for us" (Rom. 8:34). This means that heaven is on our side. Jesus is praying for us!

Jesus ascended to heaven victorious (see Eph. 4:8). When Jesus went back to heaven, He walked through the very gates of glory as the conqueror, as our victor. Dr. Vines describes the scene:

> There was a day at Calvary when all hell rode up, led by Apollyon, the great destroyer, to do battle against the Captain of our salvation. The arrows of hell pierced Him and the battle-axes of Infernity plunged themselves against Him. On and on they fought; from nine o'clock in the morning through twelve, on to three in the afternoon. But when the dust of battle settled, there was an empty tomb and our Savior, with the keys of death, hell, and the grave at His girdle! He was on His way home! He had won the victory!

> When Jesus Christ went back to heaven, His ascension gift to His church was the Holy Spirit. We have the power of the Holy Spirit today because Jesus Christ, the ascended Lord, gave it to us on the day of Pentecost. All power in the church is made possible because of the gift of the Spirit of God. All power in your individual life is possible because of the Spirit of God. He gave the gift of the Spirit, but the Bible also says He gave gifts (plural). Our Savior, our ascended Lord, gave to His church gifted men. He gave some, apostles; some, prophets; some, evangelists; some, pastors and teachers (see Eph. 4:11).

What can we say about the significance of our Lord's ascension?

1. It ended the earthly ministry of Christ. It marked the end of the period of self-limitation during the days of His sojourn on earth.
2. It ended the period of Christ's humiliation. His glory was no longer veiled following the ascension (see John 17:5; Acts 9:3,5). Christ is now exalted and enthroned in heaven (see Phil. 2:9-11).
3. It marks the first entrance of resurrected humanity into heaven and the

"Since we have a great high priest who has passed through the heavens—Jesus the Son of God—let us hold fast to the confession. For we do not have a high priest who is unable to sympathize with our weaknesses, but One who has been tested in every way as we are, yet without sin. Therefore let us approach the throne of grace with boldness, so that we may receive mercy and find grace to help us at the proper time" (Heb. 4:14-16).

beginning of a new work in heaven (see Heb. 4:14-16; 6:20). A representative of the human race in a resurrected, glorified body is the Christian's intercessor (see 1 Tim. 2:5; Heb. 7:25).

4. It made the descent of the Holy Spirit possible (see John 16:7). It was necessary for Christ to ascend to heaven in order to send the Holy Spirit.

5. It is the necessary corollary of the resurrection—the abiding proof that Jesus' resurrection was more than a temporary resuscitation. To accept the bodily resurrection but deny the ascension, someone must affirm either that Christ is still an inhabitant of earth or that He later died again.

6. It conveyed to the disciples the realization that the appearances, which had occurred at intervals over a period of 40 days, were at an end. Thus, it relieved their tension and put their minds at ease, so that, with the arrival of each new day, they did not wonder whether their Lord would reveal Himself.

7. It suggested that Jesus was no longer to be perceived by physical sensation but by spiritual insight.

8. It provided the occasion for the commissioning for witness and the promise of the Spirit (see Acts 1:1-8).

9. It provided the opportunity for our Lord to give gifted people to His church (see Eph. 4:11).

10. It provided the occasion for the promise that Jesus would come again (see Acts 1:9-11).[33]

> "He was taken up as they were watching, and a cloud received Him out of their sight. While He was going, they were gazing into heaven, and suddenly two men in white clothes stood by them. They said, 'Men of Galilee, why do you stand looking into heaven? This Jesus, who has been taken from you into heaven, will come in the same way that you have seen Him going into heaven' " (Acts 1:9-11).

This chapter has focused on seven key events in Jesus' life. Without looking back, try to name all seven.

1. _____

2. _____

3. _____

4. _____

5. _____

6. _____

7. _____

Check your work against the seven major headings in this chapter.

Jesus was born contrary to the laws of nature, reared in obscurity, and only once crossed the border of the land in which he was born and lived, and then as a child. He had no wealth or influence, neither training nor education in the world's schools. His relatives were inconspicuous and unimportant. His death was the height of shame and disgrace in His day. Yet in infancy He startled a king. As a boy He puzzled learned scholars. In manhood He ruled the course of nature. He walked on the waves and hushed the sea to sleep. He healed the multitudes without medicine and did not charge for His services.

Jesus never wrote a book; yet if everything He did were written in detail, the world couldn't contain the books that would be written. He never founded a college; yet all the schools together cannot boast of as many students as He has. He never practiced medicine; yet He has healed more broken hearts than doctors have healed broken bodies. Throughout history great men have come and gone; yet He lives on. Herod could not kill Him, Satan could not seduce Him, death could not destroy Him, and the grave could not hold Him. As King He is enthroned at God's right hand. As Priest He has atoned for sin and now prays for us. As Prophet He is the final spokesman for God.

This was the life of Jesus, and it was and still is a life like no other. After 20 centuries He is still the amazing, surprising, and fascinating Master.

Spend a few minutes reflecting on this chapter. What was the most meaningful point in your study?

_____

_____

Name something you will do to begin developing a closer walk with the Christ you encountered in this chapter.

_____

_____

End your study of this chapter by singing the hymn in the margin as your prayer to Christ.

Answers to true/false activity on page 38: 1. F, 2. F, 3. T, 4. F, 5. T, 6. F, 7. T, 8. T, 9. T, 10. F, 11. T, 12. T, 13. F

"More like the Master
 I would ever be,
More of His meekness,
 more humility;
More zeal to labor, more
 courage to be true,
More consecration for work
 He bids me do.

More like the Master
 I would live and grow;
More of His love to others
 I would show;
More self-denial, like His
 in Galilee,
More like the Master I long
 to ever be.

Refrain
Take Thou my heart,
 I would be Thine alone;
Take Thou my heart and
 make it all Thine own;
Purge me from sin, O Lord,
 I now implore,
Wash me and keep me
 Thine forevermore."[34]

Chapter 3
Fully Divine, Fully Human

Biblical teaching recognizes no difference in the Jesus who actually lived, the Jesus as reported in the Gospels, the Lord Jesus Christ of the Letters of the New Testament, and the Jesus Christ of the Christological creeds. The Jesus of history and the Christ of faith are one and the same. Certain core beliefs underlie and unite the wonderful diversity we discover in the New Testament. The view that Jesus Christ is truly God and truly man has constituted the orthodox/biblical position at least until the modern era.

The modern perspective has departed from this belief. Marcus Borg is a typical example; he says, "An older, doctrinal understanding of Christianity has ceased to be persuasive. There's been an appetite for looking at Jesus in a way that doesn't depend on Christian theological claims such as Jesus is the only begotten son of God."[1] Where might such thinking take us? In England the fallout has been tragic. *The London Sunday Times* reported that "more than 70 serving Anglican priests are members of an organization that does not believe … in the existence of God." One priest put the Christmas account on the same level as the story of Father Christmas. Stephen Mitchell, the rector of Barrow upon Soar, said, "People need to stop getting hung up about whether people are real or not. If you see a man with a white beard and a red cloak you say that's Father Christmas. That's the way I believe in Jesus Christ."[2]

This indicates the church's confusion as we move into the 21st century. However, when we read the New Testament, we quickly realize that Christology, the study of the person and work of Christ, was central not merely to the theology of the New Testament writers; it was central to the day-to-day lives of the New Testament Christians. When we say that Christology is of central importance, we affirm that Jesus Christ is like no other person who has ever existed or could exist. In declaring Christ to be fully God and yet fully man, Christianity makes claims about Him that no other religion makes about its leaders. His very nature sets Him apart from all other men. Therefore, Christianity itself is distinct from all other religions. The unique person, work, and claims of and for Jesus of Nazareth must rule out a humanistic harmony of all world faiths.

The witness of the New Testament is that God became a human being in the person of Jesus Christ. The Old Testament promised that He would come, and the New Testament testifies that He came. The New Testament

Chapter 3 Learning Goals
• **You will be able to summarize what the New Testament teaches about the person of Jesus Christ.**
• **You will express a deeper love for the Savior.**
Ask God to speak to your heart as you study this chapter.

records a rich, varied, and complementary witness to the God who took on humanity, the Word who became flesh (see John 1:14). A quintessential quartet stands out in the New Testament teaching about Jesus' deity and humanity. Those texts are John 1:1-18; Philippians 2:5-11; Colossians 1:15-23; and Hebrews 1:1-4. Their witness is majestic and awesome, and they provide for us a heaven's-eye view of Jesus.

Christians believe that Jesus is the dominant figure of the 21st century. However, the 21st-century Jesus must be the Jesus of the first century. Our ever-changing culture needs the never-changing Christ, who alone can provide both the foundation and direction for Christian faith and practice. These four pillars from the New Testament can provide stability for the church and for every believer.

The God of Incarnation: John 1:1-18

John's Gospel is important to students of Christology. It has long, discursive passages and conversations with a theological content not found in the Synoptic Gospels of Matthew, Mark, and Luke. Important for our study, John reflects an engagement with the minds of philosophers of the Greco-Roman world, setting apart John's Gospel from the Synoptic Gospels.[4]

> "In the limitless reaches of eternity, God the Father and God the Son were already there as One. Then, out of His incomprehensible love for you and me, God the Son chose to lay aside the glory of His position and all that was His in the universe in order to humble Himself and come to earth as a Man."[3]
> —*Anne Graham Lotz*

Read John 1:1-18 from several translations. Then mark each statement *T* (true) or *F* (false).

____ 1. Christ (the Word, Logos) has always existed.

____ 2. Jesus is coequal with God.

____ 3. Jesus is coeternal with God.

____ 4. Jesus is consubstantial (having the same essence or nature) with God.

____ 5. Jesus is God.

____ 6. Jesus is one with God.

____ 7. Christ created all things.

____ 8. Christ was not created.

____ 9. Christ provides true knowledge of God because He is God.

____ 10. Life itself is in Christ.

____ 11. The darkness, or evil, in the world system can never overcome the light of Christ.

____ 12. John the Baptist was divinely commissioned to tell people about Christ as the light.

____ 13. A person who has a relationship with God through Christ has life.

___ 14. A person who does not have a relationship with God through Christ is dead.

___ 15. To know God is to know Christ.

___ 16. To know Christ is to know God.

___ 17. The eternal God of the ages came to earth in human flesh.

___ 18. At His incarnation Jesus became the God-man.

___ 19. Jesus had a real, physical body; yet He was also divine.

Look for answers as you read the following paragraphs.

Christ, the *Logos* of God

Modern persons often have difficulty accepting Christ's deity. First-century persons actually had more difficulty accepting His humanity. John's prologue (see 1:1-18), as well as other parts of his Gospel, addresses both concepts in a beautifully balanced way. John clearly affirms Christ's deity. Jesus is the *Logos* (revelation/communication) of God, the Life (creation/salvation) of God, and the Light (salvation/revelation) of God.

The prologue clearly sets forth the doctrine of the incarnation, the teaching that God became man in the person of Jesus. The importance of John 1:14 can scarcely be overemphasized:

> "The Word became flesh
> and took up residence among us."

In addition, John emphasized the Son's unique relationship with the Father and provided the most significant passage in Scripture for the development of the doctrine of the Trinity. This teaching is further revealed by the upper-room discourse in John 14—16. A number of important themes are expressed there:

- The essential oneness of the Father and the Son (see 14:9-10)
- The distinctiveness of persons within the Godhead (see 14:16-18)
- The functional subordination of the Son to the Father (see 14:24,31; 16:5,28)

John called Jesus the Word, or *Logos,* in John 1:1,14. *Logos* is a word with a rich and varied history. The following have been set forth as potential sources for John's concept and usage.

Palestinian Judaism. Wisdom was often personified, and this usage was found in ancient Jewish writings outside the Bible. Here *Logos* was the wisdom or thought of God.

Greek philosophy. *Logos* represented reason, reflecting the Greek view that divinity cannot come into direct contact with evil or inferior matter. The Stoics saw *Logos* as both divine reason and reason distributed in the world

> "In the beginning
> was the Word;
> and the Word was
> with God,
> and the Word was God"
> (John 1:1).

and thus the mind. It was a creative force, the rational principle of order.

Hellenistic (Greek-influenced) Judaism. Prominent in the writings of the Greek philosopher Philo, for example, the Word was fully personified in relation to creation, being the means God employed to create the world from great waste. It was also the way God is known in the mind. However, the *Logos,* or Word, was depicted as neither personal nor preexistent.

The Old Testament. Here the Word of God is seen as—

- the agent of creation (see Gen. 1; Ps. 33:6; Prov. 8:22-29);
- the agent of revelation (see Gen. 12:1; 15:1; 22:11; Prov. 8; Isa. 9:8; Jer. 1:4; 20:8; Ezek. 33:7; Amos 3:1,8);
- eternal (see Ps. 119:89);
- the agent of redemption (see Ps. 107:20).[6]

F. F. Bruce notes, "The 'word of God' in the Old Testament denotes God in action, especially in creation, revelation, and deliverance."[7]

> Following are four ways the Word of God is used in the Old Testament. Read each of the following Scriptures and place each reference beside the point it makes: Genesis 1; Psalm 33:6; 107:20; 119:89; Jeremiah 1:4; Ezekiel 33:7; Amos 3:1.
>
> The Word of God is the agent of creation. _____
>
> The Word of God is the agent of revelation. _____
>
> The Word of God is eternal. _____
>
> The Word of God is the agent of redemption. _____

"When John calls Jesus the Word, … he is drawing attention to Jesus' greatness."[5]
—*Leon Morris*

John utilized *Logos* because of its capacity to communicate to multiple cultures—Jewish and Hellenistic (Greek). Although the term was well known, John filled it with new meaning, using it for the purpose of missions and evangelism. John's *Logos* is a person—not only God's agent in creation but also God. He is God's personal, visible (see 1:14) communication to humanity in revealing and redeeming power. The term *Logos* does not explain Jesus; Jesus explains and fills *Logos* with new meaning. Wisdom has become a person; divine reason, a man.

The Greeks were correct in affirming that we could not go up and reach the *Logos.* John said we need not despair. The *Logos* came down and lived among us. Walls notes, "It is not accidental that both the gospel and Christ who is its subject are called 'the word.' But the use of 'Logos' in the contemporary hellenistic world made it a useful 'bridge' word."[8] To the Greeks *Logos* is reason. To the Jews *Logos* is the word/wisdom. In John these ideas find new meaning as they are embodied in a person, Jesus Christ. John's use of *Logos* is cross-cultural communication of the gospel at its best.

The Word Was God

Although John 1:1 is verbally parallel to Genesis 1:1 and 1 John 1:1, the contexts of these beginnings are different. Genesis 1:1 speaks of the beginning of creation. First John 1:1 emphasizes the manifestation of God in Christ. In John 1:1 John established the preexistence of the Word in eternity past: in the beginning was the *Logos*. The *Logos* already was when the beginning took place. *Logos* refers to God's unique communication to humans. John declared that in the beginning the *Logos* existed. A time never existed when the *Logos* was not fully God.

John 1:1 affirms that Jesus is coequal, coeternal, coexistent, and consubstantial (of the same substance) with the Father. Merrill Tenney supports this understanding when he writes, "The three statements of [verse] 1 bring out ... different aspects of the nature of the Word. The first speaks of his preexistence. The second statement, 'The Word was with God,' is an assertion of the Word's distinctiveness. The preposition *pros* [translated *with*] indicates both equality and distinction of identity. [A. T.] Robertson says, 'The literal idea comes out well, 'face to face with God.' Thus this implies personality and coexistence with God. ... The third statement, 'The Word was God,' is especially significant. This is a clear statement of deity."[9]

Thus, at the very outset of his Gospel, John stated his thesis that the Word is the eternal God of the ages who came in human flesh. Tenney again helps us: "The 'Word' was deity, one with God, rather than 'a god' or another being of the same class. ... Unity of nature rather than similarity or likeness is implied. The external coexistence and unity of the Word with God is unmistakably asserted."[10] This opening verse, in a real sense, serves as the basis for all that follows in this Gospel and in another sense is the foundational pillar on which the Christian faith rests.

In verse 3 John affirmed that nothing that exists came into being except through Christ (also see Col. 1:16; Heb. 1:2). That He created all things logically and necessarily leads to the conclusion that He Himself is not created. This theological proposition is very important. F. F. Bruce notes, "When heaven and earth were created, there was the Word of God, already existing in the closest association with God and partaking of the essence of God. No matter how far back we may try to push our imagination, we can never reach a point at which we could say of the Divine Word, as Arius did, 'There was once when he was not.' "[11] Join this with the fact that a Jew like the apostle John would know the God of Genesis 1—2 only as the Creator, and we have further evidence of Jesus' full deity, evidence provided by an eyewitness at that.

Verse 5 affirms that this God is light and can never be conquered: it keeps on shining (present tense). *Darkness,* a word John used to identify evil in the

"All things were created
   through Him,
and apart from Him not
   one thing was created
that has been created.
In Him was life,
and that life was the light
   of men.
That light shines
   in the darkness,
yet the darkness did
   not overcome it"
(John 1:3-5).

world system, which opposes the true God, attempts to overcome or comprehend the light, but it fails. Christ, as the light, provides true spiritual illumination and true knowledge of God because He is God. John the Baptist was divinely commissioned to attest to the truth about Christ the *life* (a word occurring 36 times in John's Gospel) and Christ the *light* in order that people might believe (see vv. 6-9).

To understand what John was saying here, we must appreciate his unique use of the word *life*. When John spoke of life and death, he most often used these terms to describe someone's relationship with God. Someone who has a relationship with God (through Christ) has life because he knows God, who is life. A person who does not have a relationship with God (is separated from Christ) is dead because he does not know God. To know God is to know Christ and to experience the life of God.

One of John's favorite terms is *martureo,* used 47 times in his writings and translated *witness, testimony,* or *record.* In this Gospel seven persons, things, or events "bear witness to"—attest, substantiate—the truth of Christ's claims:
1. The Father (see 5:37; 8:18)
2. Christ Himself (see 8:14,18,37)
3. The Spirit (see 15:26; 16:14)
4. The works of Jesus (see 5:36; 10:25)
5. The Scriptures (see 5:39)
6. John the Baptist (see 1:6-8)
7. Other people (see 4:39; 12:17; 15:27).
John teaches us that the Son was the true Light who came into the world. To *believe* (used almost one hundred times in this Gospel and always as a verb) or to receive Him as *Logos* and life is to know God in the truest sense and to enjoy the privilege of being His child (see 1:12). Indeed, we can truthfully know God by no other means than Jesus. As our Lord Himself affirmed in 14:6, " 'I am the way, the truth, and the life. No one comes to the Father except through Me.' " Jesus Himself excluded any type of universalism, which claims that eventually all people will be saved, or inclusivism, which claims that people can be saved by Jesus without personally trusting Him.

The Word Became Flesh
Perhaps the heresy of Gnosticism or Docetism necessitated verse 14. Gnosticism, from the Greek word *gnosis,* meaning *knowledge,* taught that salvation is by mystical knowledge and that the material world is inferior or evil. *Docetism,* meaning *to appear,* said Christ was a phantom or mystical spirit who did not have a physical body. Both false teachings denied the genuine, permanent reality of the incarnation by which God took humanity on Himself.

"The Word became flesh and took up residence among us.
We observed His glory, the glory as the One and Only Son from the Father,
full of grace and truth"
(John 1:14).

Record the way each Scripture shows that Jesus was truly human.

John 4:6-7 _____

John 11:35 _____

John 12:27 _____

John 13:21 _____

John 19:28-30 _____

John 19:32-34 _____

John 19:38-42 _____

John insisted that the Word became not only truly God but also truly human. John recorded that our Lord was tired and thirsty (see 4:6-7), wept (see 11:35), was troubled in spirit (see 13:21), and bled and died (see 19:30). Without becoming less than God (see Phil. 2:5-11), the Son took on Himself complete humanity, apart from sin (see 2 Cor. 5:21; Heb. 4:15). John affirmed that He "became flesh." At His incarnation God did not become man; He became God-man. The words "took up residence among us" can be understood to mean "pitched his tent" or "tabernacled among us." Just as the Hebrew word *shekinah (glory)* indicates that the bright cloud of God's glorious person settled on the tabernacle (see Ex. 24:16; 40:35), in Christ God's glorious person dwelt among people, and they beheld, gazed on, and examined His glory.[12]

There was never a time when the Son did not exist. In the incarnation the Son became Jesus, the second person of the triune God, the God-man. The One who was from all eternity in the most intimate and personal relationship with the Father has declared, explained, and made known the Father (see John 1:18).

Go back and check your answers to the true/false activity on pages 52–53. All of the statements are true.

Write a paraphrase of John 1:14 that an older child could understand.

_____

"No one has ever seen God. The One and Only Son— the One who is at the Father's side— He has revealed Him" (John 1:18).

The God of Humiliation: Philippians 2:5-11

The Christ hymns of the New Testament provide insight into the theology and worship of the early church. Many students of the Bible believe that, in addition to John's prologue, at least the following should be recognized as early confessional/worship hymns to Christ: Ephesians 2:14-16; Philippians 2:6-11; Colossians 1:15-20; 1 Timothy 3:16; Hebrews 1:13; and 1 Peter 3:18-22. The rich Christological content of the hymns teaches us that very early in the history of the church, the believing community had a very high Christology in its praise, worship, and teaching. Christians already viewed Jesus as God and man. Insufficient time elapsed between the Christ-event and the composition of these hymns for embellishment, myth, and fanciful elaboration to take place, as modern critics assert.

Philippians 2 stands out for its significance in constructing a biblical Christology. This particular passage is especially noted for two important aspects of Christology:
1. The *kenosis* doctrine: the emptying of Christ as God the Son became a man
2. The hypostatic union: the uniting of two natures in one person

The Mind of Christ

Paul authored this Christ hymn or possibly adapted an existing hymn to teach the Philippians about the person of Christ. The primary intent is ethical, teaching us how to live the mind of Christ through Christ's example: "Make your own attitude that of Christ Jesus" (Phil. 2:5). This text also addresses theological questions about Christ's role in our redemption.[14]

The hymn is arranged in a simple form of two stanzas:
1. Christ's humiliation—verses 6-8
2. Christ's exaltation—verses 9-11

The hymn's ethical context is shown in verses 1-5. Paul urged the Philippians to have the attitude, or mind, of Christ. Verse 5 literally reads, "Think you," a present imperative of command. This command follows a call to unity (see v. 2), humility (see v. 3), and sensitivity (see v. 4). Humility, above all, is identified as the character trait that best exemplifies the mind of Christ. Therefore, the hymn of 2:6-11 actually serves as a divine illustration of the mind of Christ, the mind the believer should pursue and cultivate. Believers need to express genuine concern and compassion for one another, which is possible only by adopting the same mind or attitude (disposition) we discover in Christ. Christ's demonstration of self-disregard, concern, and compassion is the theme of this Christ-hymn.

"Christ's self-emptying is the supreme example of humility. To have the mind of Christ, we must deliberately humble ourselves by becoming other-directed, first to God and then to others."[13]
—*T. W. Hunt*

Read Philippians 2:5-11. The application of these verses is found in Philippians 2:1-5. Read these verses, noting especially verses 3-5. Summarize in your own words what verses 3-5 teach.

_____

_____

What is one way you can apply this teaching in your home?

_____

In the Form of God

For Paul, like John, the starting point is Christ's preexistence. Philippians 2:6 reads, "… who, existing in the form of God. …" *Existing* emphasizes continued existence. Christ exists. He always has, in the realm of eternity, forever. He always is (see John 8:58). There was never a time when He was not. He is eternally existent. By definition this means He is God.

The word translated *form* in verse 6 is *morphe*. Scholars have proposed the following meanings of this word.
1. The essential nature and character of God
2. The mode of being or way of being
3. The image of God (a second-Adam Christology; see Gen. 1:26-27)
4. The glory of God (viewed as a continuation of John's theology; see John 17:5)
These four options are quite similar in meaning, and each highlights a truth about Jesus taught in the Bible. Still, let's do our best to get at the idea Paul was teaching. A word study of *morphe* is a good place to start. The word *morphe,* which can mean *form, shape, appearance,* or *essence,* "refers to that form which truly and fully expresses the being which underlies it." Hence the idea "does not refer simply to external appearance but pictures the preexistent Christ as clothed in the garments of divine majesty and splendour."[15] *Morphe* identifies Jesus with the essential nature and character of God. The idea is that of "outward display of an inner reality or substance." Rogers and Rogers say, "Here it refers to the outward display of the divinity of the preexistent Christ, in the display of His glory as the image of the Father."[16] Therefore, a combination of views 1 and 4 above is what Paul was saying. Paul affirmed that Christ eternally exists in the very nature, essence, essential being, and glory of God. Whatever God is, Christ is, in all of God's glory! *Morphe* pictures Christ as possessing the permanent, unchangeable pattern of deity.

> "… who, existing in the form of God, did not consider equality with God as something to be used for His own advantage …" (Phil. 2:6).

An Advantage Not to Be Used

Although Christ has always existed as God, He

> did not consider equality with God
> as something to be used for His own advantage (v. 6).

This phrase looks back to the expression "existing in the form of God." Fiercely debated, it may mean that His equal status and privileges with God were not things He violently sought to seize or believed He must forcibly retain. The word *grasped* (NIV), is *harpagmos,* which can mean (1) robbing or (2) a prize gained through robbery.[17] Being coequal and coeternal with God by the very nature of His being, Christ did not have to forcibly strive for equality with God, as if He did not possess it, nor did He have to forcibly assert that equality, as if He could lose it. Bruce notes, "There is no question of Christ's trying to snatch or seize equality with God: that was already his because he always had the nature of God. Neither is there any question of his trying to retain it by force. The point is rather that he did not treat his equality with God as an excuse for self-assertion or self-aggrandizement; on the contrary, he treated it as an occasion for renouncing every advantage or privilege that might have accrued to him thereby, as an opportunity for self-impoverishment and unreserved self-sacrifice."[18]

The Form of a Slave

Christ grasped not sovereignty but service, giving up His high and lofty position for the salvation of souls and the pleasure of the Father. He did not grasp but gave. He did not climb but condescended. Verse 7 says, "He emptied Himself." The crucial word is *kenoo,* meaning *to empty.* Verses 7-8 express a clear understanding of what it means that Christ "emptied Himself":

- He assumed the form of a servant.
- He took on the likeness and external form of a man.
- He humbled himself (see vv. 2-4).
- He became obedient to the point of death.
- He died on a cross, a death of ultimate humiliation.

These verses express the idea that there was an emptying by addition. The Son did not surrender His deity but added humanity. Further, the type of humanity He added was not that of a sovereign but that of a servant or slave. He received not a crown but a cross. F. F. Bruce says it well: "It was in the manner of his death, his death on the cross, that the rock bottom of humiliation was reached. ... By the standards of the first century, no experience could be more loathsomely degrading than that."[19] However, we must main-

"Instead He emptied Himself by assuming the form of slave, taking on the likeness of men. And when He had come as a man in His external form, He humbled Himself by becoming obedient to the point of death— even to the death on a cross" (Phil. 2:7-8).

tain a nonnegotiable truth: "He emptied Himself" does not mean that Christ ceased to be deity. Christ voluntarily became subordinate in function or assignment but not in His essence. His divine nature remained the same.

Yet a real emptying took place. In His High Priestly prayer our Lord says,

"Father, glorify Me in your presence
with that glory I had with You before the world existed" (John 17:5).

Jesus did not surrender His deity, but He surrendered His glory. He became in a sense God incognito. He willingly laid aside, in humble obedience to the Father, the praises, position, and prerogatives of heaven. In humiliation Jesus totally reversed the priorities and principles of this world system.

The wedding of deity and humanity was permanent. The Son is now forever the God-man. The emptying, however, was only for the time of incarnation. Christ temporarily laid aside the free, voluntary exercise of the rights and privileges of deity. His emptying, therefore, involved self-limitation as well as ultimate humiliation. Christ partook of unglorified humanity. He voluntarily forfeited, for a time, the free use of His divine attributes, depending instead on His Father and the Holy Spirit.

Highly Exalted

God did not leave the drama unresolved. In exalting Jesus, the Father affirmed His pleasure in His Son. The contrast between the way humanity treated Jesus and the way God the Father treated Jesus is instructive:

- Humanity gave Jesus a cross, but God gave Him a crown.
- Humanity gave Jesus a grave, but God gave Him back His glory.
- Humanity gave Jesus anguish, but God gave Him adoration.
- Humanity expelled Jesus, but God exalted Jesus.
- Humanity gave Jesus thorns, but God gave Him a throne.

Verses 9-11, therefore, affirm a threefold exaltation of the Savior:

1. An exalted position (see v. 9)
2. An exalted adoration (see v. 10)
3. An exalted confession (see v. 11)

These verses note the consequent action of God the Father in light of the Son's voluntary obedience and humiliation by death on a cross. "Highly exalted" (v. 9) means *to exalt above and beyond, to superexalt.* No doubt Paul had in mind here our Lord's resurrection, ascension, and present position in heaven.

"Gave Him the name" (v. 9) may refer to the name Yahweh, Lord, or Jesus. The latter seems more likely, though merit lies in all three options. The bowing of adoration (see v. 10) and the word of confession (v. 11)

"For this reason God also
   highly exalted Him
and gave Him the name
   that is above every name,
so that at the name of Jesus
   every knee should bow—
of those who are in heaven
   and on earth and under
   the earth—
and every tongue should
   confess that Jesus Christ
   is Lord, to the glory of
   God the Father"
(Phil. 2:9-11).

emphasize the deity and universal lordship of the Son, a reality that glorifies the Father. Verse 10 echoes Isaiah 45:23. In Isaiah Yahweh is in view; in Philippians it is Jesus. The verse ascribes to Jesus that which is ascribed to the God of the Old Testament. All will bow (see v. 10). Nothing in all of creation is outside the lordship and authority of the Lord Jesus Christ. Bruce notes:

> "Jesus (Christ) is Lord" is the quintessential Christian creed, and in that creed "Lord" is given the most august sense that it can bear. When Christians in later generations refused to say "Caesar is Lord," they refused because they knew that this was no mere courtesy title that Caesar claimed: it was a title that implied his right to receive divine honors, and in this sense they could give it to none but Jesus. To them there was "only one God, the Father, ... and ... only one Lord, Jesus Christ" (1 Cor. 8:6). In the Greek [Old Testament] Gentile Christians read, Yahweh was denoted either by *theos* ("God") or (most often) by *kyrios* ("Lord"); they reserved *theos* regularly for God the Father and *kyrios* regularly for Jesus. When divine honors are thus paid to the humiliated and exalted Jesus, the glory of God the Father is not diminished but enhanced. When the Son is honored, the Father is glorified; for none can bestow on the Son higher honors than the Father himself has bestowed.[21]

It is necessary that Christ should be both God and man. Only as a man could He be a redeemer for humanity; only as a sinless man could He fittingly die for others. Only as God could His life, ministry, and redeeming death have infinite value and satisfy God's demands to deliver others from sin. People need a God-man, and He is Jesus Christ, the second person of the Trinity.

> Read again from your Bible Philippians 2:5-11. Spend a few minutes reflecting on the lordship of Christ. Sing the chorus in the margin. If you don't know the tune, make up your own!

The God of Creation: Colossians 1:15-23

The church very early determined its position on the doctrine of Christ. Contemporary denials of Christ's deity or manhood or another aspect of His person and work are really no different from the heresies the early church confronted. Colossians 1—2 has played a significant role in the battles the church has fought in the area of Christology. T. L. Trevethan writes: "The foundation of the argument of the letter to the Colossians is found in 2:9-10.

"He is Lord, He is Lord!
He is risen from the dead
and He is Lord!
Ev'ry knee shall bow,
ev'ry tongue confess
That Jesus Christ is Lord."[20]

The gospel, Christian truth, has its source in Jesus. He is the crown of God's revelation because 'in him the whole fulness of deity dwells bodily' [Col. 2:9]. There is no stronger statement of the full deity of our Lord Jesus in the Scripture."[22] And F. F. Bruce adds about this Christ hymn: "This is one of the great Christological passages of the [New Testament], declaring as it does our Lord's divine essence, pre-existence, and creative agency."[23]

Why did Paul write to the Colossians? Probably because their world was not much different from our own in religious and spiritual climate. The Colossians were beset by a fusion of religious teachings. Three streams of teaching flowed into the area of the Lycus Valley where Colossae was located:

- *Greek thought.* Hellenistic, or Greek, beliefs usually fostered a dualistic view of the universe (material versus spiritual), leading to either asceticism (strict self-denial) or libertinism (lack of moral restraint).
- *Mysticism.* The local pagan climate included superstitious occultism (the practice of rites to influence supernatural powers) with mystical rites (practices that attempt to bring people into direct contact with and experience of the supernatural).
- *Legalistic Judaism.* The Judaistic influences were particularly rigid and austere, breeding extreme asceticism.

These three streams blended together into a pseudophilosophical soup of mystery cults.[24] The Colossian Christians must have wondered how Christ fit into such a worldview. They continually faced pressure to mix the pure gospel of Christ with the religious and philosophical teachings of the surrounding culture—to practice a blended Christianity. Paul reminded these believers of the lordship of Jesus Christ, His preeminence, and the work He had accomplished for them. He warned them against human religion and instructed them in proper Christian conduct in light of the true gospel. Paul wanted these believers to have an "assured understanding, and have the knowledge of God's mystery—Christ" (Col. 2:2).

The Image of the Invisible God

Many New Testament scholars believe that Colossians 1:15-20 is an early Christian hymn exalting the Son as the supreme Lord. Verse 15 begins with the affirmation that Christ is the "image of the invisible God." The Greek word for *image, eikon,* means *likeness, representation, image, form, manifestation,* and *reflection.* Here and in 2 Corinthians 4:4 the word is used to convey a precise and absolute correspondence. Jesus Christ is the perfect, visible manifestation of the invisible God.

Eikon does not imply a weak imitation or a feeble copy of something. It implies the outward manifestation and illumination of something's inner

"He is the image of the invisible God, the firstborn over all creation, because by Him everything was created, in heaven and on earth, the visible and the invisible, whether thrones or dominions or rulers or authorities— all things have been created through Him and for Him. He is before all things, and by Him all things hold together" (Col. 1:15-17).

core and essence. The word involves the twin ideas of representation and manifestation. Jesus is the representation and manifestation of God, who is invisible. John Calvin provides a valuable commentary on this verse: "[Paul] calls Him the image of the invisible God, meaning by this, that it is in him alone that God, who is otherwise invisible, is manifested to us. ... Christ is called the image of God on this ground—that He makes God in a manner visible to us. ... We must, therefore, beware of seeking Him [God] elsewhere, for everything that would set itself off as a representation of God apart from Christ, will be an idol."[26]

The idea of perfection does not lie in the word *eikon* itself but must be sought from the context. Here *eikon* means that Christ is essentially and absolutely the perfect expression and representation of God the Father. Christ is the image of God in the sense that He perfectly reveals God's nature and being. Adam was created *in* God's image, but Christ *is* God's image. He brings to light and makes knowable the God who, both to our physical and inward eyes, is invisible. Jesus is the person and "portrait of God."[27]

Paul's point, then, is simple. If you want to see and know God, then look at and believe in Christ. Christ is not simply a picture of what God is like; He is truly God Himself. As Jesus Himself said, " 'The one who has seen Me has seen the Father' " (John 14:9), and " 'before Abraham was, I am' " (John 8:58). Colossians 1:15 is an explicit affirmation of Christ's divine essence. Paul affirmed Christ as Lord God, both of the cosmos—His material creation—and the church—His spiritual creation. In verse 20 he applied Christ's lordship to the individual believer.

Lord of Creation

Christ is called the firstborn (see v. 15). This word conveys the ideas of primacy, priority, and supremacy—of priority in time and supremacy in rank. To understand this term, particularly as it is applied to Christ, we must rid our minds of the idea that Christ is somehow the first of a long succession of creatures. As we have seen and shall see again, Christ is not a creature. He is the Creator Himself. The term *firstborn* points to Christ's preeminence and preexistence. *Firstborn* originally referred to the first son of a family who inherited the rights of the family—its name, property, and other privileges. In some cases his position as firstborn made him uniquely eligible to be the king. For example, Psalm 89:27 points to the Davidic Messiah's special position of honor.[28]

In verse 15 Paul had in mind that Christ is God the Father's first and only Son. This use compares to John's use of "One and Only" in John 1:14,18; 3:16 (NIV). The idea is not that Christ was ever somehow born to God but rather that in His relationship to the Father in the Trinity He enjoys all of the rights

"The staggering, breathtaking truth is that every single item in the cosmos owes not only its origin but also its continuing existence to the one whom we know as Jesus Christ."[25]

—*James I. Packer*

and privileges the Father bestows on Him. These include the right to oversee the creation of all things—a creation that was created by Him, for Him, and in Him. He is creation's conception, continuance, and consummation.

In Colossians 1:16-17 *firstborn* obviously carries the nuances of supremacy and preeminence. Christ is the source-agent and preserver of creation and is worthy of all honor. Christ as sustainer ("by Him all things hold together," v. 17) makes the universe a cosmos instead of a chaos. These verses explicitly affirm Christ's divine function or divine works in creation. Christ is the Creator, preeminent over every creature. A Jew like Paul could conceive of God only as Creator. Further, because Christ created "all things" (v. 17), He Himself must be uncreated, or the statement is untrue.

Christ is not God's greatest creation through whom all else came into existence. He is the Creator, and by Him all that is, came into existence. Notice that the word *created* occurs twice in verse 16. The first looks back to the act of creation, while the second affirms that the creation still remains a testimony, monument, and proof of His creative might. Therefore, Christ is God. He is preexistent and preeminent over all creation as its God.

Lord of the Church

Christ is also the head of the body, the church (see v. 18). The church owes Him exclusive allegiance, complete devotion, and total obedience. This type of commitment is reserved only for God and thus for Christ because He is God. Paul affirmed Christ's deity from every direction. To be the head of the church is to be its directing brain—its sovereign, chief, and leader. He guides and governs it. The pronoun *He* is emphatic, indicating that Christ and no other is the head. He alone is the church's Lord and Ruler.

Notice that the term *firstborn* again appears in verse 18: "He is the beginning, the firstborn from the dead." *Beginning* can mean *supremacy in rank, precedence in time,* or *creative initiative.* All three ideas apply here, though *creative initiative* seems to be the idea Paul intended to convey.[29]

We saw that *firstborn* refers to Christ's position as Creator of all things. The word denotes source and preeminence. Here it refers to the fact that Jesus conquered death in His resurrection. He is sovereign even over death. His resurrection is His claim to be the head of the church. Obviously, for Paul the resurrection of Jesus is not optional: "If there is no resurrection of the dead, then Christ has not been raised; and if Christ has not been raised, then our preaching is without foundation, and so is your faith" (1 Cor. 15: 13-14). Paul would not accept the judgment of the Jesus Seminar, which has denied Jesus' bodily resurrection, or of Rudolf Bultmann, who repeatedly denounced the doctrine of resurrection.

"He is also the head of
the body, the church;
He is the beginning, the
firstborn from the dead,
so that He might come
to have first place in
everything.
For God was pleased
to have all His fullness
dwell in Him"
(Col. 1:18-19).

Though we will devote an entire chapter to the subject of the resurrection, R. Albert Mohler, Jr., gets to the heart of this issue: "Paul sets himself—and the true Church—over against Bultmann, the Jesus Seminar, and all who deny or deride the empty tomb. Either the tomb is empty, or our faith is in vain. Paul wants nothing to do with Bultmann's effort to find a spiritual meaning without a historical event, nor with the Jesus Seminar's anti-supernaturalism. ... Paul cared deeply about whether the tomb was empty."[30] Paul's point is that Christ has full rights over the church because He conquered the great enemy of His people, death. In so doing, He proved Himself to be God! Hence, verse 18 sums up the matter: Christ should "have first place in everything!"

Verse 19 explains that in Christ we see the very essence of God. "All His fullness" means that Christ lacks nothing of what it means to be God. He possesses all of God's attributes (saving grace, love, goodness, light, omniscience, and so on). Paul used the word *fullness,* probably a technical term in the vocabulary of false teachers, eight times in this letter. It has the sense of *undiluted, unalloyed;* Christ is pure deity—the sum total of all the divine power and attributes. "Nothing of deity is lacking in Christ."[31]

The words "dwell in Him" mean *to be at home permanently, to reside.* There was never a time when Christ did not possess deity; He was and is always God.

Colossians 2:9 expands and supplements 1:19. "In Him" is emphatic and exclusive, again affirming the incarnation. "The entire fullness" emphasizes comprehensiveness and completeness, reiterating that Christ is completely God; there is nothing about Christ that is not God; there is nothing about God that Christ is not.

"In Him ... God's nature dwells" means that Christ is in His essence God. In 2:9 Paul took the expression of Christ's deity one step further than in 1:19 by linking it with Christ's incarnation in the word *bodily.* Paul's point here is that Christ is fully God and fully man. This verse is therefore one of the New Testament's best verses to show both Christ's deity and Christ's humanity and to show that He is both fully God and fully man at the same time.

Lord of the Christian

In Colossians 1:20-23 Paul went on to apply the doctrine he had presented to the Colossian believers. First he explained that Christ, the mediator, has reconciled the Colossian Christians to God, despite their initial hostility and sin, by His blood. Second Corinthians 5:17-21 states that reconciliation transforms people; appeases God's wrath; and comes only through Christ, the sinless substitute. Paul also declared that Christ can be counted on to take

"In Him the entire fullness of God's nature dwells bodily" (Col. 2:9).

the Colossians on to a complete spiritual transformation so that they would become acceptable to the Father. Their responsibility was to continue in the faith as they originally heard it and believed it and not to fall away into errors that result when Christianity is blended with other beliefs. "Holy" (v. 22) means *consecrated and dedicated, separated from sin and to the Savior for His service and sanctifying work.* "Faultless" (v. 22) means *without blemish.* "Blameless" (v. 22) means *above reproach, unreprovable.* Therefore, Christ's preeminence is of the utmost importance to the personal lives and destiny of the Colossian believers, as well as to those of believers today.

Colossians 1—2 declares that Christ is God. The key verses 1:15,19; and 2:9 reveal that Christ is fully and completely God. Because of Jesus' resurrection, His lordship is expressed in terms of His victory over death and His vindication by God. This lordship extends to creation itself. Nothing exists outside the sovereign lordship of Christ.

The God of Revelation: Hebrews 1:1-4

An old Puritan preacher said he needed to know only two things: (1) Does God speak? (2) What does God say? To these two excellent questions I would add: (3) Is Jesus God's final Word? We find the answer to all three of these questions in the opening verses of the Book of Hebrews, our fourth great Christological text.

Hebrews is a finely crafted series of sermons. An overriding theme links its 13 chapters together: Jesus is God's very best. The word *better* or *superior* occurs 19 times in the New Testament, 13 of those in Hebrews. As we mine the wealth of this book, we discover that Jesus—
- is better than the angels (1:4);
- provides a better hope (7:19);
- provides a better covenant (7:22; 8:6);
- provides better promises (8:6);
- provides a better sacrifice (9:23);
- provides a better possession (10:34);
- provides a better country (11:16);
- provides a better resurrection (11:35);
- provides a better blood testimony (12:24).

The author of Hebrews believed that Jesus is the best that God could give. Therefore, in Christ's coming, God speaks, He speaks clearly, and He speaks with finality. What was God saying when He sent His Son from heaven to earth? Hebrews 1:1-4 says several crucial things.

"God was pleased to have all His fullness dwell in Him, and to reconcile everything to Himself through Him by making peace through the blood of His cross—whether things on earth or things in heaven. And you were once alienated and hostile in mind because of your evil actions. But now He has reconciled you by His physical body through His death, to present you holy, faultless, and blameless before Him—if indeed you remain grounded and steadfast in the faith, and are not shifted away from the hope of the gospel that you heard" (Col. 1:19-23).

To Hear God, Listen to Jesus

Read Hebrews 1:1-2. What were some ways God spoke to people in the Old Testament?

_____

_____

How does God speak to us today? _____

_____

"Long ago God spoke to
the fathers by the prophets
at different times and in
different ways. In these last
days, He has spoken to us
by His Son, whom He has
appointed heir of all things
and through whom
He made the universe"
(Heb. 1:1-2).

"Long ago God spoke" (v. 1). Immediately we are confronted with both God's reality and activity. God has continually talked to His people throughout history. How did God speak?

- To Adam and Eve He spoke directly in the cool of the day.
- To Abraham He spoke directly in visions and in a visit.
- To Jacob He spoke in a dream.
- To Moses He spoke in a burning bush and face-to-face, as one person speaks to another.
- To Elijah He spoke in a still, small voice.
- To Isaiah He spoke in a grand vision in the temple.
- To Hosea He spoke through family tragedies.
- To Amos He spoke in a basket of summer fruit.[32]

God spoke through visions and dreams, the Urim and Thummin. He spoke through angels, natural events, and pillars of fire. He spoke in history and psalms, proverbs and prophecy. "God spoke ... at different times and in different ways" (1:1). "God spoke," and because it was God speaking, it was true; and because it was at different times and in different ways, it was partial, progressive, and fragmented. What He gave the fathers and prophets was inerrant but incomplete. It was promise, not fulfillment. According to His providential plan, it was partial, step-by-step, elemental, and preparatory.

When we learn to read, we first learn letters, then words, then sentences, then paragraphs, then stories, then books. God instructed humanity the same way. He began simply, progressively. He began with the good but saved the best for last. God's revelation through His prophets was true but partial.

In contrast, God's revelation through His Son is true and perfect (see 1:2). "Last days" speaks of the final age, the messianic age since the cross. *Spoken* is the same word as in verse 1. The same God spoke, but in verse 2 there is a difference in time (last days) and quality (His Son). The coming of the Son brought to completion and fulfillment all that the Old Testament predicted and promised about the Messiah. God spoke by His Son. And in His Son God came down; God came near. If you want to hear God, listen to Jesus.

To See God, Look at Jesus

Jesus is the invisible God made visible. When we look at Jesus, we are looking at God. If we look carefully and closely, exactly what do we see? Hebrews provides us with seven glorious affirmations of God's final answer.

Jesus is the divine Inheritor (see Heb. 1:2). "Whom He has appointed heir of all things" looks to the future. *Appointed* emphasizes God's divine will and intention. "Heir of all things" is a title of dignity. Christ has the supreme place in all creation. God has only one Son, and He has given Him everything. The Father delights to honor the Son. Not a beautiful rose or a majestic peak, not a radiant sunset or a single drop of the sea belongs to anyone other than Jesus. You too are not your own (see 1 Cor. 6:19-20).

Jesus is the divine Creator (see Heb. 1:2). "Through whom He made the universe" addresses the Son's role in creation. All three members of the triune God are active in creation. The Father is the author, the Son is the administrator, and the Holy Spirit is the agent. This verse focuses attention on the Son. Through Him the Father literally made the universe. Here the sum total of all the various periods of time is intended, and how appropriate that word is for the Son.[33] It has been well said, "History is His story." From Genesis to Revelation, from the Garden of Eden to the Island of Patmos, all of Scripture and all of history are about Jesus.

Jesus is the divine Revealer (see Heb. 1:3). "He is the radiance of His glory" tells us the Son is the shining forth of brightness from within, or the reflection, a shining forth of brightness, from without. He is the outshining of God's glory or the reflection of God's glory. Whichever is the case, and the former is the better option, in Jesus, the Son, we see the true and authentic glory of God. As Jesus Himself said in John 14:9, " 'The one who has seen Me has seen the Father.' " Put those words in the mouth of any other, and they are foolishness. But put them in the mouth of Jesus, and you have nothing less than God's final answer. As the sunlight is to the sun, so the eternal Son is to the Father.[34]

Jesus is the divine Character (see Heb. 1:3). "The exact expression of His nature" teaches that "the Son is the perfect representation of God's being."[35] "Exact expression" translates a single Greek word found only here in the New Testament. Originally, it meant an instrument of engraving and then the mark stamped by that instrument. Jesus is the very stamp of God's

"In these last days, He has spoken to us by His Son, whom He has appointed heir of all things and through whom He made the universe. He is the radiance of His glory, the exact expression of His nature, and He sustains all things by His powerful word. After making purification for sins, He sat down at the right hand of the Majesty on high" (Heb. 1:2-3).

nature, the precise impression or mark.[37] Whatever makes God, God, the Son is all of it as well. If God is omnipotent, the Son is omnipotent. If God is omnipresent, the Son is omnipresent. If God is omniscient, the Son is omniscient. If God is eternal, the Son is eternal. If God is immutable (unchanging), the Son is immutable. If God is holy, just, righteous, and love, the Son is holy, just, righteous, and love. When you see Jesus, you see who God really is. This is not true of Buddha, Muhammad, Confucius, Moon, the Dalai Lama, or any other person of history. Jesus Christ, God's Son, alone reveals to us exactly what the Father is like.

Jesus is the divine Sustainer (see Heb. 1:3). "He sustains all things by His powerful word" emphasizes the present. "Sustains" means *carries along.* He created it, He maintains it, and He is carrying it toward its appointed goal. Note that the verse says "all things," not some things. Nothing is excluded either on a global scale or on a personal one. The Son has a vital interest in this world He made and loves. Through His powerful, enabling, active word He spoke the worlds into existence, and by that same word He sustains the worlds until their proper end.

Jesus is the divine Redeemer (see Heb. 1:3). He made "purification for sins." Because our greatest need was forgiveness, God sent us a Savior. Jesus did what no forefather or prophet could ever do. He did what no apostle or angel could ever do. He did what only He could do. He took care of our sin.

Purification is the Greek word *katharismos.* It means *to cleanse, purge, or purify.* This is why Jesus is God's final answer. He cleansed us of sins (see 1:3), He made a satisfaction for sins (see 2:17), He put away sins (see 8:12; 10:17), He bore our sins (see 9:28), He offered a sacrifice for sins for all times (see 10:12), He made an offering for sin (see 10:18), and He annulled sin by His sacrifice (see 9:26). Whatever the sin is, He has defeated it.[38]

The word *making* means *provided,* and here it affirms a once-for-all, completed action in the past. The purpose for which Jesus came was not to be admired in a Christmas cradle. The purpose for which He came was to make atonement on Calvary's cross by His blood. All of humanity had a heart problem, not a physical one but a spiritual one. We needed divine cleansing. Jesus, God's final answer, did that for us all.

Jesus is the divine Savior (see Heb. 1:3). "Sat down at the right hand of the Majesty on high" speaks of Jesus' exaltation in heaven following His perfect work of redemption. Hebrews 10:12 says, "This man, after offering one sacrifice for sins forever, sat down at the right hand of God." The Lord has completed His work of salvation. Unlike a priest's work under the old covenant, the work of atonement is now finished. No chair was found in the holy of holies, for the work was never finished. More sacrifices always needed

"The Son of God became man that the children of men might become children of God."[36]

—Martin Lloyd-Jones

70

to be made. Not so with the Son, God's final answer. He is at the right hand of God, the Majesty on high. He is sitting, resting in the position of greatest honor because His work of atonement is complete.

To Worship God, Lift Up Jesus

The Bible does not support the ideas of religious pluralism and multiple ways to God. It offers only one way to the Father. We come by way of the Son, God's final answer. This Son is to be worshiped, honored, lifted up. Why?

Jesus is not an esteemed servant (see Heb. 1:4,13-14). In the first century as in the 21st, people were confused about the proper place of angels. In verse 4, for the first of 13 times, the author of Hebrews used the word *higher* to put angelology in correct perspective. Mentioned 105 times in the Old Testament and 165 in the New Testament, angels are ministering spirits for the saved (see 1:14). Though they are good, they are not the best. They are servants, but Jesus is sovereign (see 1:7). They are creatures, but Jesus is the Creator. They are workers, but Jesus is worshiped (see 1:6). They are esteemed servants, but Jesus is superior.

Jesus is the exalted Son (see Heb. 1:4-14). Angels are called servants. Jesus is called Son. Angels continue to serve God. Jesus is now seated beside God. "Name" in verse 4 connotes all that a person is in character and conduct. In all respects Jesus is better—better in His person (He is God), better in His work (He dealt with sin once and for all), and better in His position (at God's right hand). God has many servants but only one Son. His name is Jesus.

> "He became higher in rank than the angels, just as the name He inherited is superior to theirs. Now to which of the angels has He ever said:
> 'Sit at My right hand until I make Your enemies Your footstool?'
> Are they not all ministering spirits sent out to serve those who are going to inherit salvation?"
> (Heb. 1:4,13-14).

Summarized below are key beliefs about Jesus Christ held by two major cults: Jehovah's Witnesses and the Church of Jesus Christ of Latter-Day Saints (the Mormon church). Think about what you have learned as you read these false beliefs.

Jehovah's Witnesses
- Jesus was first created by God and then was used by God to create all other things.
- Jesus is a lesser god than the Father.
- Jesus and the archangel Michael are the same being.
- Jesus was just a man, nothing more, while He was on earth.
- Jesus died on a stake as a man, not as the divine Son of God.
- A physical resurrection did not occur; Jesus was raised a spirit-creation.
- The Trinity is a Satanic lie.

The Church of Jesus Christ of Latter-Day Saints
- Jesus is not eternally God.
- Jesus was begotten as a spirit-child of God.
- Jesus was the spirit-brother of Lucifer.
- Jesus progressed as a spirit-son until He became a god.
- Jesus was born on earth through a physical relationship between a flesh-and-bone Heavenly Father and Mary.

Suppose that a member of one of these groups asked you, "What do you believe the New Testament teaches about Jesus Christ?" Write your response, using extra paper if needed.

_____

_____

_____

_____

_____

_____

What was the most meaningful thing you learned from your study of this chapter? It may have been a Scripture or a statement you read, or it may have been a thought God placed in your heart.

_____

_____

_____

End your study of this chapter by singing the song in the margin. Let it express your renewed love for the Savior.

"There is a name I love
   to hear,
I love to sing its worth;
It sounds as music
   in my ear,
The sweetest name
   on earth.

Oh, how I love Jesus,
Oh, how I love Jesus,
Oh, how I love Jesus,
Because He first loved me."[39]

Answers to true/false activity on page 52: all of the statements are true.

Chapter 4
No Other Name, No Other Way

Jesus Christ, the Son of God, was born to die. Unlike any other person who has ever lived, Jesus came into this world for the express purpose of dying on a cross as the perfect sacrifice for the sins of the world (see 1 John 2:2; 4:10). First John 4:14 states, "The Father has sent the Son as Savior of the world." John Stott, in his classic work *The Cross of Christ,* emphasized, "Evangelical Christians believe that in and through Christ crucified God substituted himself for us and bore our sins, dying in our place the death we deserved to die, in order that we might be restored to his favour and adopted into his family."[1] This reconciliation between God and humans, accomplished by Jesus' substitutionary death on the cross, is known as the atonement.

When we consider Jesus' death on the cross, several questions come to mind. Why did Jesus have to die? What was Jesus' crucifixion like? What did Jesus' death accomplish? By virtue of His atoning death on the cross, is Jesus the only way to heaven? We will seek to answer these important questions in this chapter.

Why Did Jesus Have to Die?

Jesus had to die for two basic reasons: the sinfulness of humanity and the holiness and justice of God. Romans 3:23 contains both truths: "All have sinned and fall short of the glory of God." By Jesus' substitution of Himself for us on the cross, God "demonstrated His righteousness at the present time, so that He would be righteous and declare righteous the one who has faith in Jesus" (Rom. 3:26). Let's look at the first condition that required the coming of God's Son for the salvation of sinners.

The Sinfulness of Humanity
Men and women are created in God's image. However, the entrance of sin into the world has had great and terrible consequences on God's creation, especially on humans. The sin of Adam and Eve (see Gen. 3) was not a moral lapse. They deliberately disobeyed God and rejected Him. The day they disobeyed God, they died spiritually, which ultimately brought physical death as well (see Gen. 2:17). Examining the consequences of the fall will help us understand why Jesus died.

Chapter 4 Learning Goals
- **You will be able to explain in your own words why Jesus died on the cross.**
- **You will commit to share the message of the cross with someone who has never trusted Christ.**

You are halfway through the study. Thank God for His guidance to this point. Ask Him to speak to your heart as you study this chapter.

Read Romans 1:18—3:20; 5:12-21; and Ephesians 2:1-22. List all the results of the fall of humankind you can find.

_____

_____

_____

Check your work as you read the following paragraphs.

Paul described some of the consequences of the fall in Romans 1:18—3:20; 5:12-21; and Ephesians 2:1-22. Important among these consequences are the effects of sin on our will, which is the volitional, or decision-making, element in us. Although we still function as free moral agents with free will, our decisions and actions are always influenced by our sinful nature.

Because sin entered the world and we inherited Adam's sinful nature (see Rom. 5:12-19), we are by nature hostile to God and estranged from Him (see Rom. 8:7; Eph. 2:1-3). We have wills that do not obey God, eyes that do not see God, and ears that do not hear God. Spiritually, we are dead to God. We are indeed enemies of God (see Col. 1:21). We cannot genuinely repent or turn to God without divine enablement, because we are by nature hostile to Him (see Rom. 3:9-20).

"The mind-set of the flesh is hostile to God because it does not submmit itself to God's law, for it is unable to do so" (Rom. 8:7).

An awareness of these ideas helps correct frequent misunderstandings about the nature of sinful humanity. As a result of the fall, humans are totally depraved. *Totally* does not mean that every person commits every sin or that every person, or any person, is as evil and wicked as possible. Rather, total depravity suggests that no part, function, activity, or state of a person escapes the corruption of sin. The effects of sin have touched every component of our being. People can still do good things as viewed by society, but these thoughts and actions, no matter how well intended, are sinful if not done for the glory of God. People can choose to do good but not the ultimate good, which is to please God and seek his eternal glory. Thus, depravity describes our total, willful rejection of the will and glory of God.

Total depravity means (check the correct statements)—
❑ a person is as morally debased and corrupt as possible;
❑ every person in the world is affected by sin and is a sinner;
❑ a person commits every possible sin;
❑ no part or state of a person can escape the corruption of sin.
Check your work in the previous paragraphs.

As a result of sin, God's image was not lost (see Gen. 9:6; Jas. 3:9) but was severely damaged and marred. As a result, "all our righteous acts are like filthy rags" in God's sight (Isa. 64:6), and all of us are spiritually dead and alienated from God (see Eph. 2:1-3). We are unable to reflect properly the divine image and likeness (see Rom. 1:18-32). The components of that image—rulership over creation, relationships with God and others, and resemblance to God—were all damaged and marred by the fall.

Rulership over creation. Humanity's role of exercising dominion over creation (see Gen. 1:28) was drastically disturbed by the effects of sin on humans and by the curse on nature. Humanity still had authority to rule over creation, but this sovereignty was substantially restricted and set in a different context (see Gen. 3:17-19). God changed the relation of the earth to humans. Now they would be forced to extract from the earth the necessities of life by strenuous exertion, striving against an alienated and rebellious earth. Humans in their disordered state would never subdue the earth as God intended. The ground became a reminder of the fall, and the curse struck at the heart of our responsibility, our work, and our provision.

Relationships with God and others. Humanity's ability to live in proper relationships has been corrupted. On the human level the simple gender distinctions within "one flesh" (Gen. 2:24) were twisted to become oppositions and opponents. Whereas marriage was formerly a fully loving personal relationship, it became dominated by selfish urges and a desire to dominate and ruthlessly control. Childbirth continued but with pain as a reminder of the consequences of sin. The potential for selfishness in human relationships points to sin's malignant presence in all of life.

Humanity's relationship with God was also severely damaged. The original relationship of peace and mutual love was lost. The fear, the hiding, and the full awareness of sin's consequences (see Gen. 3:10-11) reveal the effect of the insecurity and anxiety of fallen humanity. This insecurity, with its counterpart, pride (self-assertion), is a tragic combination. However, the disruption of the communion between God and humans has not destroyed our need and desire for that fellowship.

Resemblance to God. Humanity is marred both in its spiritual and physical aspect. In its spiritual aspect humanity is damaged in three ways.

1. Our intellect is disordered; we are often mistaken as to matters of fact and flawed in our reasoning. We still have the ability to think as a dimension of God's image. However, sin interferes with our thought processes, so that we make incorrect decisions by means of erroneous thinking.

2. We inherit a corrupted will. Sin predisposes humans to voluntarily make choices that oppose the revealed will of God.

> " 'Cursed is the ground
>   because of you;
> through painful toil
>   you will eat of it
> all the days of your life.
> It will produce thorns
>   and thistles for you,
> and you will eat the plants
>   of the field.
> By the sweat of your brow
>   you will eat your food' "
> (Gen 3:17-19).

3. We are morally corrupted. At the fall, humans obtained full knowledge of good and evil, and with that knowledge we also came under bondage to evil and sin.

In our physical aspect humanity also suffered corruption through the fall. The toil and sweat of life will end in the dust of death (see Gen. 3:19). Humanity (the image of God), when alienated from God, is merely dust without animation—dust in the wind.

However, there is good news in the midst of this loss and sorrow. Fallen people are still inherently valuable because they still possess the divine image (see Gen. 1:26-31). God as Savior did not leave Adam and Eve and their descendants under the curse of judgment and death but proclaimed the promise of the Seed of woman, who would restore to them what they had lost (see Gen. 3:15; Gal. 4:4-5). This Conquering Seed had God's image in the same sense that God had originally intended for Adam and Eve. Unlike the man and the woman, the Seed used the image to choose God's will instead of the lies of the evil one (see Matt. 4:1-11; Phil. 2:6-11).

Resemblance restored. The New Testament clearly designates Jesus Christ as the Conquering Seed. Christ is the exact image of God. In calling Christ the image of God (see Col. 1:15), Paul emphasized God's nature and personality in the image, revealing Christ as the visible expression of the invisible God. Christ restored the resemblance aspect of God's image and provided correct knowledge about God.

Rulership restored. Christ also restored the rulership aspect of God's image. Christ is the head of the body, the new final authority that God has placed in creation. As humans were to fulfill the role of master of the old creation, Christ is the head of the new creation, the church. Christ rules now in the hearts of His people, who are extending His kingdom through the preaching of the gospel. This kingdom will be fully realized in all of its glory on earth during the millennium, when Christ comes the second time to claim what rightfully belongs to Him (see 1 Cor. 15:20-28; Rev. 20:1-6).

Relationship restored. Finally, Christ restored the relational aspect of God's image. Christ succeeded in re-creating the loving, fruitful relationship God intended at creation. In Christ we can love God and one another as originally intended.

God's image is restored in fallen people when we accept Christ by faith (see 2 Cor. 5:17). Our experience of salvation and our growth in Christlikeness reverse the corruption of God's image in us. When we leave this earth to live with God forever, His image in us will be complete, perfect, redeemed, and fully restored because Christ lives in us.[2]

> **"When the completion of the time came, God sent His Son, born of a woman, born under the law, to redeem those under the law, so that we might receive adoption as sons"** (Gal. 4:4-5).

God's Holiness and Justice

Now we will turn our attention to the other reason Jesus had to die. Jesus' death addressed the issues of divine holiness and justice.

The Bible teaches us that our God is holy. First Peter 1:15-16 states, "As the One who called you is holy, you also are to be holy in all your conduct, for it is written, 'Be holy, because I am holy.' " Jesus taught, " 'Be perfect, therefore, as your heavenly Father is perfect' " (Matt. 5:48). God loves sinners, but He hates sin. Because our God is holy, pure, righteous, and just, both in His character and His ways, He has an abiding wrath directed toward sin. Paul wrote, "God's wrath is revealed from heaven against all godlessness and unrighteousness of people who by their unrighteousness suppress the truth" (Rom. 1:18). God does not laugh or wink at sin, any sin. He despises it and finds it worthy of the judgment of eternal, spiritual death.

Humanity's great offense requires a great recompense. God's perfect justice demands that every sin be punished. God would have been just to destroy the entire human race for its sin. Yet in His goodness, mercy, love, and compassion He sent a Savior. The violent, vicarious death of the sinless, spotless Son of God on the cross turned the wrath of Holy God away from wicked sinners. Rather than pour out His wrath and judgment on us, God instead, in the fullest measure, poured it out on His Son. Christ's death satisfied the offended holiness and glory of God for sinners.

Jesus frequently emphasized that His death was necessary for the salvation of humanity.

- When Peter tried to save Jesus after His arrest, Jesus asked, " 'Do you think that I cannot call on My Father, and He will provide Me at once with more than 12 legions of angels? How, then, would the Scriptures be fulfilled that say it must happen this way?' " (Matt. 26:53-54).
- At Caesarea Philippi Jesus "began to teach them that the Son of Man must suffer many things, and be rejected by the elders, the chief priests, and the scribes, be killed, and rise after three days" (Mark 8:31).
- At the empty tomb the angel reminded the women, " 'He is not here, but He has been resurrected! Remember how He spoke to you when He was still in Galilee, saying, "The Son of Man must be betrayed into the hands of sinful men, be crucified, and rise on the third day"?' " (Luke 24:6-7).
- In John 12:24 Jesus provided a rationale for the nature of the atonement: " 'Unless a grain of wheat falls into the ground and dies, it remains by itself. But if it dies, it produces a large crop.' " Only by dying can the grain produce fruit.

To Jesus' words we can also add the observation of the author of Hebrews:

> "The good news is not just that God became man, nor that God has spoken to reveal a proper way of life to us, or even that death, the great enemy, is conquered. Rather, the good news is that sin has been dealt with."[3]
> —*James Montgomery Boice*

> **"The death of Christ is sufficient for all sinners who have ever lived, for it was not merely a finite human, but an infinite God who died."[4]**
> —*Millard J. Erickson*

"Almost everything is purified with blood, and without the shedding of blood there is no forgiveness" (Heb. 9:22). All of these verses show that the atonement was necessary to fulfill the Scriptures.

Calvin wrote, "It was also imperative that he who was to become our Redeemer be true God and true man. It was his task to swallow up death. Who but the Life could do this? It was his task to conquer sin. Who but very Righteousness could do this?"[5] The Son of God had to come. The Son of God had to die. God's holiness demanded satisfaction. God's love sent a Savior.

Jesus died for two basic reasons. Name them.

1. _____

2. _____

If you had difficulty, review "Why Did Jesus Have to Die?"

What Was Jesus' Crucifixion Like?

God sent His Son to die, and the means of His death was crucifixion. All four Gospels record the passion of our Lord, providing significant detail about the enormous suffering and torture He endured. Other Christian, Jewish, and Roman sources provide additional insight about scourging and execution on a cross. These details help us realize all that Jesus suffered for us.

After Jesus and His disciples had observed Passover, they traveled to the Mount of Olives, which was northeast of the city and near Gethsemane (see Luke 22:39-46). Jesus, knowing that the time of His death was near, suffered great mental anguish, and as described by the physician Luke, "His sweat became like drops of blood" (22:44). Although this is a rare phenomenon, "bloody sweat (hematidrosis or hemohidrosis) may occur in highly emotional states or in persons with bleeding disorders. As a result of hemorrhage into the sweat glands, the skin becomes fragile and tender. Luke's description supports the diagnosis of hematidrosis."[6]

Sometime after midnight the temple officials, accompanied by a mob, arrested Jesus at Gethsemane (see Matt. 26:47). They took Him to Annas and then to Caiaphas, the Jewish high priest. Jesus was tried before the Sanhedrin and was found guilty of blasphemy. The guards then blindfolded Jesus, spit on Him, beat Him, and slapped Him.

The Jews viewed blasphemy as a crime punishable by death. However, permission to execute a criminal had to come from the Romans. Jesus was taken early in the morning to Pilate, not as a blasphemer but as a self-proclaimed king who would undermine Roman authority. Pilate, unable to bring charges against Jesus, sent Him to Herod Antipas. Herod also made no official charges and returned Jesus to Pilate. Pilate again could find no basis to charge Jesus, but the people demanded His crucifixion. Pilate finally granted their demand and handed over Jesus to be flogged (scourged) and crucified (see Matt. 27:15-25).

For about 12 hours (between 9:00 p.m. Thursday and 9:00 a.m. Friday) Jesus suffered great emotional stress (as evidenced by hematidrosis), abandonment by His disciples, and a severe physical beating. He also experienced a traumatic, sleepless night and had to walk more than 2.5 miles to and from the sites of the various trials. These physical and emotional stresses probably made Him more vulnerable to the effects of the scourging.

Scourging usually preceded a Roman execution. The normal instrument was a short whip called a flagellum. It was composed of several single or braided leather thongs of variable lengths, in which small iron balls or sharp pieces of sheep bones were tied at intervals. The man was stripped, usually completely naked, and his hands were tied to a post. The back, buttocks, and legs were beaten or flogged, either by two soldiers called lectors or by one soldier who alternated his position from one side to the other. The scourging was intended to punish and weaken the victim to a state just short of collapse or death. Some persons, in fact, died from scourging.

As the soldiers repeatedly struck the victim's back, the iron balls would cause deep cuts or contusions, and the leather thongs or sheep bones would cut deep into the skin. As the beating continued, "the lacerations would tear into the underlying skeletal muscles and produce quivering ribbons of bleeding flesh. Pain and blood loss generally set the stage for circulatory shock."[7] The amount of blood loss probably determined how long the victim would survive on the cross.

Because this was a Roman scourging, we cannot be certain that the number of lashes was limited to 39, which was the limit set by Jewish law. The soldiers mocked Jesus by placing a robe on Him, a crown of thorns on His head, and a wooden staff as a scepter in His right hand (see Matt. 27:27-31). When the soldiers tore the robe from Jesus' back, they probably reopened His wounds, again causing our Lord excruciating pain.

"The severe scourging, with its intense pain and appreciable blood loss, most probably left Jesus in a preshock state. Moreover, hematidrosis had rendered his skin particularly tender. The physical and mental abuse meted out by the Jews and the Romans, as well as the lack of food, water, and sleep, also contributed to his generally weakened state. Therefore, even before the actual crucifixion, Jesus' physical condition was at least serious and possibly critical."[8]

> **"God proves His own love for us in that while we were still sinners Christ died for us!" (Rom. 5:8).**

Crucifixion, which probably began with the Persians, was perfected by the Romans as a form of torture designed to produce a slow death with maximal pain and suffering. It was one of the most humiliating and cruel forms of execution. Roman law protected Roman citizens from crucifixion, except perhaps in the case of the desertion of a soldier.[10]

The condemned man was forced to carry on his shoulders his own cross-bar (called a patibulum) from the place of his scourging to the place of his crucifixion. He was usually naked unless prohibited by local customs. The processional to the place of crucifixion was led by a military guard, who would not leave the site until they were sure that the victim was dead. To prolong the crucifixion, a wooden block, serving as a crude seat, was often attached midway down the main vertical post. At the place of execution the victim was thrown to the ground with his arms outstretched. The hands were nailed or tied to the crossbar. The Romans appear to have preferred nailing.[11]

After the hands were nailed and the arms were fixed to the crossbar, the victim was lifted onto the main post. The feet were then nailed to the cross. The soldiers and the crowd often taunted and jeered at the victim, and Scripture indicates that Jesus' crucifixion was no different (see Matt. 27: 39-44). Survival on the cross lasted from three or four hours to three or four days, depending on the severity of the scourging. However, the Roman soldiers sometimes hastened death by breaking the legs below the knees.[12] It was common for insects to light on or dig into the open wounds, the eyes, the ears, and the nose of the person on the cross. Even birds would sometimes tear at a victim's wounds. To ensure that the victim was dead, the guards often pierced the body with a sword or a spear (see John 19:34).

What would a medical analysis of this treatment reveal? Scourging served to weaken the condemned man. Blood loss probably continued throughout the crucifixion. The wrists were nailed to the cross to support the weight of the body hanging from them. The probability of painful injury is certain. "The driven nail would crush or sever the rather large sensorimotor median nerve. The stimulated nerve would produce excruciating bolts of fiery pain in both arms."[13] When the feet were nailed to the front of the cross with an iron spike through the first or second intermetatarsal space, numerous nerves would have been injured.[14]

In addition to excruciating pain throughout the body, respiration, particularly exhalation, was impaired. People did not die from blood loss when crucified. They died from asphyxiation.

The weight of the body, pulling down on the outstretched arms and shoulders, would tend to fix the intercostal muscles in an inhalation

> "On a hill far away stood
>   an old rugged cross,
> The emblem of suff'ring
>   and shame;
> And I love that old cross
>   where the dearest and best
> For a world of lost sinners
>   was slain."[9]

state and thereby hinder passive exhalation. … Adequate exhalation required lifting the body by pushing up on the feet and by flexing the elbows and adducting the shoulders. However, this maneuver would place the entire weight of the body on the tarsals and would produce searing pain. Furthermore, flexion of the elbows would cause rotation of the wrists about the iron nails and cause fiery pain along the damaged median nerves. Lifting of the body would also painfully scrape the scourged back against the rough wooden stipes. Muscle cramps and paresthesias of the outstretched and uplifted arms would add to the discomfort. As a result, each respiratory effort would become agonizing and tiring and lead eventually to asphyxia.[15]

Death by crucifixion was the most horrible death imaginable; yet that is what the Son of God endured for sinners like you and me.

After being scourged and mocked, at about 9:00 a.m. Jesus was taken to be crucified. He was so weak that He could not carry the crossbar from the Praetorium where He was scourged to the site of crucifixion approximately ⅓ mile away.[16] Simon of Cyrene was made to carry Christ's cross, and the processional made its way to Golgotha (see Mark 15:21-22). Here Jesus and two thieves were crucified. He was taunted throughout the crucifixion. He spoke seven times from the cross. Because speech requires exhalation, these short, terse utterances must have been particularly difficult and painful. At about 3:00 p.m. that Friday, Jesus cried out in a loud voice and died (see Matt. 27:50). Jesus' body was taken down from the cross and placed in a tomb (see Matt. 27:57-61).

These are the terrible, tragic facts of Jesus' death. However, the marvelous accomplishments of that death are the occasion for worship and thanksgiving.

Read again this section, "What Was Jesus' Crucifixion Like?"

Now read aloud Luke 22:39—23:49 slowly and with meaning.

Charles Wesley wrote more than 6,500 hymns. He wrote everywhere: at home, at church, in town, in the country, walking down the street or in fields, even on horseback! God gave him the gift of expressing our faith in lyrical form. Read in the margin some words from one of Wesley's hymns.

Stop and pray, thanking God for Jesus' suffering and sacrifice on Calvary to pay for your sins.

"And can it be that I should gain An int'rest in the Savior's blood? Died He for me, who caused His pain? For me, who Him to death pursued? Amazing love? how can it be That Thou, my God, should die for me?"[17]

What Did the Cross Accomplish?

Understanding what Jesus' death on the cross accomplished has occupied the attention of the church throughout all of its history. A number of theories of the atonement have been proposed through the years. It will be helpful to point out the strengths and weaknesses of these theories before examining the most satisfying explanation of the atonement—as penal substitution.

Theories of the Atonement

The recapitulation theory. Irenaeus of Lyons (A.D. 130–202) proposed that Christ recapitulated, or summarized, in Himself all the stages of human life, including the aspects that relate to us as sinners. Irenaeus wrote, "He [Christ] summed up in himself the long line of the human race, procuring for us salvation thus summarily, so that what we had lost in Adam, that is, the being in the image and likeness of God, that we should regain in Christ Jesus."[19] In essence, Christ reversed the course for humankind that Adam had set us on.

Irenaeus was correct in saying that Christ reversed our course, but He never became a sinner. Furthermore, this theory does not take into account other biblical characteristics of the atonement.

Ransom-to-Satan (also called classic or dramatic) theory. This theory, set forth by Origen of Alexandria (A.D. 185–254), viewed Christ's death as a ransom paid to the devil. Through the fall Satan had obtained certain rights over humanity, which Christ annulled by ransoming us. By an almost holy deception God defeated the devil. Illustrations of the fishhook (Gregory of Nyssa) and the mousetrap (Augustine) were employed to advance this theory. Rufinus of Aquileia (c. A.D. 400) reproduced Gregory's illustration and shows us how this view was understood: "The purpose of the Incarnation ... was that the divine virtue of the Son of God might be as it were a hook hidden beneath the form of human flesh ... to lure on the prince of this age to a contest; that the Son might offer him his flesh as a bait and that then the divinity which lay beneath might catch him and hold him fast with its hook."[20]

This theory falters in that God owes Satan nothing. However, this erroneous view would be the dominant understanding of the atonement for almost one thousand years.

The satisfaction theory. This view, developed by Anselm of Canterbury (1033–1109), would become extremely important in the church's understanding of the atonement. Sin, as an offense against God's honor and majesty, cannot go unpunished if satisfaction to God is not made. Humans are indebted to God, and God's justice demands satisfaction. God resolved the dilemma by means of the incarnation of the God-man, Jesus Christ.

"The core of the gospel is assuredly that Christ Jesus came to save sinners."[18]
—*Benjamin B. Warfield*

"God will not do it, because he has no debt to pay; and man will not do it, because he cannot. Therefore, in order that the God-man may perform this, it is necessary that the same being should be perfect God and perfect man, in order to make this atonement [satisfaction]. For he cannot and ought not to do it, unless he be very God and very man."[21]

Anselm rightly stressed atonement as the goal of the incarnation, a satisfaction to God, and a substitution. His theory is foundational to an understanding of the atonement as penal substitution.

The moral-influence theory. This view, popular among liberal theologians today, was first articulated by Peter Abelard of Paris (1079–1142). He saw nothing in the divine nature that requires satisfaction. In this view, God requires not justice but repentance. The work of Christ consists of providing an example and teaching about God's love, which inspires and awakens in us a reciprocal love. Christ's life and sufferings were intended to exert a moral impression on hard hearts, melting them into sorrow and repentance, which then find favor in God's love. Christ's example moves us to love God, who in turn forgives us on the basis of that love.

Abelard's view of the atonement rightly stresses God's love, but it misses the biblical balance of God's holiness.

The example (also called Socinian) theory. This theory, which originated in the late 16th century and was popularized by Unitarians, has also been favored by liberal theologians. Adherents to this view hold that Christ's death did not atone for sin. By His teaching in life and His example in death, Christ brought salvation to humanity. Sin is not as serious as is commonly believed, and God, by an act of His will, may simply choose to forgive. Christ's death is not a substitution but a moral stimulus. Christ gave us an example of how to love God, and by His death He inspired us to do so.[22]

This theory confuses the accomplishment of the atonement with our response to it. It is also flawed from the start because it denies Christ's deity.

The governmental theory. Hugo Grotius (1583–1645), a lawyer, proposed that Christ suffered not to pay for the sins of humankind or to give us an example but to show that, although God was willing to forgive, He still considered the transgression of the law a serious matter. By His death Christ demonstrated the high estimate God placed on His law and government. Christ died as a public example of the depth of sin and the length to which God would go to uphold His moral law.[23]

This theory is deficient in ignoring that Jesus died in the place of sinners. It also denies that God requires personal accountability for sin, claiming instead that God can simply choose to forgive us without demanding payment for our sin.

"In Him we have redemption through His blood, the forgiveness of our trespasses, according to the riches of His grace that He lavished on us with all wisdom and understanding" (Eph. 1:7-8).

The mystical theory. With the coming of the Enlightenment, rationalism, and antisupernaturalism, Christ was humanized, and His work was reevaluated. The father of liberal theology, Friedrich Schleiermacher (1768–1834), began his theology with humanity, emphasizing a subjective feeling of god-consciousness. He defined *religion* as *the feeling of absolute dependence.* Christ's sufferings for our good should fill us with love, with a god-consciousness. The purpose of the incarnation was the deification of humanity. Jesus was the mirror of divinity who awakens the divine consciousness within all who meet Him. Schleiermacher rejected any idea that Christ's death satisfied God's demand for justice. Christ's death simply exercises influence to change people. Christ's unbroken unity with God enabled Him to bring a potential mystical influence for good to people through His death.

This theory falters in denying Christ's deity, unduly exalting fallen humanity, and making no attempt to deal with Scripture.

The Nature of the Atonement as Penal Substitution

Each of the previous theories contains elements of truth, some more than others. However, when we carefully examine the whole of redemptive history and crucial theological terms found in Scripture, we reach an inescapable conclusion. The death of God's Son on the cross accomplished a penal satisfaction or penal substitution for sinners. The word *penal* refers to legal punishment that is due. The Lord Jesus, by offering Himself as a sacrifice, by substituting Himself for us, and by actually bearing the punishment that should have been ours, satisfied God's holiness, righteousness, and justice and achieved a reconciliation between God and humanity. Jesus took our place, bore our sin, became our curse, endured our penalty, and died our death.[25]

This view is firmly rooted in the testimony of Scripture. Christ's life and death certainly exemplified divine love and exerted an influence for good by providing a model of servanthood and sacrifice. But more importantly, Christ's death provided for sinners a sinless, substitutionary sacrifice that satisfied divine justice. He made redemption available that delivers us from slavery to sin, reconciles us to God, and restores us to full fellowship and inheritance in the household of God.

Several beautiful images in Scripture highlight the various components of Christ's saving work.

Atonement. The idea of atonement is the focal point of the scriptural idea of Christ's saving work (see Isa. 53:10; Rom. 3:25; Heb. 2:17; 1 John 2:2; 4:10). Atonement can be rightly understood only in light of God's holiness and justice. God's justice is the severity of the reaction of His holiness to sin. This concept affirms both that God's holiness had to be satisfied and that the sins

"In Jesus we meet God, face to face, and through him our sovereign and great God has taken triumphant action against sin, death, and the devil by yielding himself in substitution for his people on the cross."[24]
—*David F. Wells*

of humanity had to be removed. Atonement was realized when God Himself took on Himself, in the person of Jesus, the sinfulness and guilt of humankind in order to execute His justice and to forgive their sins. God was moved to this self-sacrifice by His infinite mercy, love, and compassion.

Propitiation. The crucial word *propitiation* appears in four important texts: Romans 3:25; Hebrews 2:17; 1 John 2:2; 4:10. *To propitiate* means *to appease or satisfy.* Humans were in no way involved in the act of propitiation. In the act of atonement God satisfied Himself through the sacrifice of His Son. God was in Christ reconciling the world to Himself (see 2 Cor. 5:18). J. I. Packer says it beautifully:

> Christ's death had its effect first on God, who was hereby propitiated (or, better, who hereby propitiated himself), and only because it had this effect did it become an overthrowing of the powers of darkness and a revealing of God's seeking and saving love. The thought here is that by dying Christ offered to God satisfaction for sins, satisfaction that God's own character dictated as the only means whereby his "no" to us could become a "yes."[26]

Redemption. The idea of redemption is vitally related to the themes of liberation, deliverance, and ransom. Redemption is a metaphor from the world of commerce, war, and slavery. *To redeem* normally means *to pay a ransom price for the release of a captive or a slave.* However, at some places in Scripture the word *redeem* suggests a different idea. Sometimes it refers to a free man who is purchased or redeemed to be a slave of Christ.

A struggle is taking place between the kingdom of God and the hostile, demonic powers enslaving humankind. Redemption is the idea of bringing sinners out of such hostile bondage into authentic freedom. As Redeemer, Jesus broke the power of sin and set sinners free. He created a new, obedient heart by delivering us from the power of sin, guilt, death, and Satan. He gathered a people who have been bought with a price, the precious blood of Christ (see 1 Pet. 1:18-19). Central texts that highlight redemption include Mark 10:45; Galatians 3:13; and 1 Timothy 2:6.

Reconciliation. Reconciliation looks at Christ's atonement through the picture of battle or broken relationships. It involves bringing fallen humanity out of alienation into a state of peace and harmony with God. Jesus, as Reconciler, healed the separation and brokenness created by sin and restored communion between God and humankind. Reconciliation is not a process by which people become more acceptable to God but an act by which we are delivered from estrangement to fellowship with God. In Christ "God was

"God presented Him as a propitiation through faith in His blood, to demonstrate His righteousness, because in His restraint God passed over the sins previously committed" (Rom. 3:25).

"We know that no one is justified by the works of the law but by faith in Jesus Christ" (Gal. 2:16).

reconciling the world to Himself, not counting their trespasses against them" (2 Cor. 5:19). Because of Christ's work on the cross, God has chosen to treat us as His children rather than as sinners and transgressors (see 2 Cor. 5:18-21; Eph. 2:12-16; Col. 1:20-22).

Justification. Justification looks at our relationship through the metaphor of law. To justify is to declare righteous. It is a judicial term indicating that a verdict of acquittal has been announced. There is no longer any condemnation. The claims of God's law against the sinner have been fully satisfied. Key texts include Romans 3:28; Galatians 2:16; 3:11. Romans 3 connects our justification to the propitiation or atonement of Jesus (see Rom. 3:25).

Justification does not alter God's righteous demands, for in Christ all of His demands have been fulfilled. Christ's perfect life of obedience to the law and His atoning death that paid sin's penalty are the bases for our justification (see Rom. 5:9).

God declares us justified in His sight, a standing of righteousness before Him. In Romans 3 this justification is said to be apart from the law (see v. 21), through faith in Christ (see v. 22), to all who believe (see v. 22), by grace (see v. 24), through payment by Christ (see v. 25), by means of satisfaction or propitiation (see v. 25), by blood (see v. 25), and in perfect justice (see vv. 25-26).

Match each of the following terms with its correct description.

____ 1. Justification
____ 2. Redemption
____ 3. Reconciliation
____ 4. Atonement
____ 5. Propitiation

a. Sinners are delivered from the bondage of sin and are set free from the power of sin, guilt, death, and Satan.

b. We are delivered from estrangement and are brought into fellowship with God.

c. The righteous demands of a holy God were fully satisfied by the sacrifice of His Son.

d. Because of Christ's death on the cross, God declares us righteous and no longer under condemnation.

e. God took on Himself, in the person of Jesus, humanity's guilt to execute His justice and forgive our sins.

Summarizing what Jesus accomplished on the cross, Packer makes nine observations about the atonement:

1. God "condones nothing" but judges all sin as it deserves, which Scripture affirms and our conscience confirms to be right.

2. Our sins merit ultimate penal suffering and rejection from God's presence (conscience also confirms this), and nothing we do can blot them out.

3. The penalty due to us for our sins, whatever it was, was paid for us by Jesus Christ, the Son of God, in His death on the cross.

4. Because this is so, we through faith in Him are made "the righteousness of God in Him" (2 Cor. 5:21). That is, we are justified; pardon, acceptance, and sonship become ours.

5. Christ's death for us is our sole ground of hope before God. Christ fulfilled the demands of God's justice and underwent the wrath due us.

6. Our faith in Christ is God's own gift to us, given in virtue of Christ's death for us; that is, the cross procured it.

7. Christ's death for us guarantees our preservation to glory.

8. Christ's death for us is the measure and pledge of the love of the Father and the Son to us.

9. Christ's death for us calls and constrains us to trust, to worship, to love, and to serve.[27]

Other religions have a martyr, but Jesus' death was that of a Savior. It provides salvation from our sins because Christ took our place and died our death. By His obedient life He fulfilled the law for us, and by His death on the cross He satisfied the demands of the law for us. The cross of Christ is the execution of justice for God's unrelaxed penalty revealed in the law (see Gal. 3:10-13). In Jesus God's holy love is revealed. His holiness is satisfied, and His love is demonstrated (see 1 John 4:10). Hallelujah! What a Savior!

> "Love consists in this: not that we loved God, but that He loved us and sent His Son to be the propitiation for our sins" (1 John 4:10).

Is Jesus the Only Way?

The religious climate today is similar to that of the first century A.D. When Jesus was born in Bethlehem, the Roman Caesar claimed to be God. Augustus was deified and worshiped by his subjects across the far-flung Roman Empire. The early church came into existence and moved out in its missionary outreach across the Mediterranean world in the midst of a plethora of religions. The Pantheon in Athens was full. Roman and Greek gods and goddesses were worshiped, and Artemis and other Eastern mystery religions were popular. The astrology of Egypt and Babylonia held sway over the lives of many people. Into this diverse culture the early Christians carried the message that Jesus and Jesus alone saves.

Today the claim that Jesus is the only way to God is not popular, because the Western world is characterized by an intellectual, philosophical, and cultural outlook called postmodernism. Rejecting all absolutes, postmodernism asserts that there is no absolute truth; rather, truth is an individual determination. Holding that all worldviews are equally valid and no one worldview more true than any other, postmodernism values experience over reason. Postmodernism challenges authority and hierarchies of power structures, rejects the doctrines and practices of biblical Christianity, and rewrites or "deconstructs" much of history. This philosophy denies objective reality while embracing pluralism and diversity.

Our postmodern culture is receptive to new religions and diverse beliefs and practices, and dozens vie for people's allegiance. Here is a capsule of five belief systems, some old, some new, that are growing in numbers and influence in this country.

Islam. Islam is a monotheistic faith that offers Allah as the only true God. He is sometimes portrayed as merciful and compassionate. Yet a careful investigation of the Qur'an finds Allah to be distant and harsh. Islam is founded on a works salvation that keeps a careful tally of good and bad deeds. Little grace is found in this God and little mercy in this religious system.

Buddhism and Hinduism. These two ancient religions have branched out from their Indian roots and have found fertile soil in Western culture. Buddhism sees our problems as suffering, rather than sin, and desire, which is the root cause of suffering. Salvation is obtained by self-effort as a person seeks to abolish desire. The goal through a series of reincarnations is to reach nirvana, which is escape from the cycle of life, death, and rebirth. Actor Richard Gere is a leading public-relations figure for Buddhism in America.

Hinduism teaches self-deification and promotes pantheism, the concept that everything is God or part of God. The holistic health doctor Deepak Chopra is a leading proponent of Hinduism in American culture. Both Hinduism and Buddhism embrace the concepts of reincarnation and karma. Reincarnation is the belief in the preexistence of souls and their rebirth over and over again as various persons through history. Karma is the belief that a person reaps in this life what was sown in the past life, good or bad.

Transcendental Meditation, which comes from Hinduism, offers participants spiritual growth, peace, and happiness from focusing on a mantra, a word or phrase that a leader gives to each person.

New Age. An eclectic mixture of beliefs and practices from many religions and movements, including Buddhism and Hinduism, the New Age Movement has become a major phenomenon. Thirty years ago books on this movement began to appear on shelves in bookstores; later, entire sections in bookstores were devoted to the movement. Now entire bookstores are devoted to New Age literature.

Monism and pantheism are key ideas in New Age beliefs. Monism is the belief that all is one and that humans are one with nature and one with God.

> **"It's obvious why Eastern religion is such an attractive form of salvation for a post-Christian culture. It soothes the ego by pronouncing the individual divine, and it gives a gratifying sense of 'spirituality' without making any demands in terms of doctrine or ethical living."[28]**
> *—Charles Colson*

Pantheism is the belief that everything is God, including plants, rocks, and humans. Enlightenment comes as persons realize that they are God and undergo a change in consciousness. Reincarnation and karma are key beliefs of New Age. Actress Shirley MacLaine, with her media presence, books, and lectures, has popularized New Age thinking and beliefs.

Channeling is a New Age practice involving spirit possession. A medium goes into a state of altered consciousness and communicates teachings to listeners. Crystals are considered sources of healing, power, and energy.

The occult. Occultism is a growing phenomenon that comprises many diverse concepts and practices. Astrology teaches that planets and stars determine a person's fate. People read horoscopes in newspapers not just for amusement but as a serious endeavor to understand life and the future. Divination, the art of divining or foretelling the future, uses tools like Tarot cards and Ouija boards. Spiritualism promotes communication between the dead and the living, using mediums and séances. Witchcraft and Satanism are not confined to secret meetings but are openly practiced.

How do followers of these religions and movements view the person and work of Jesus Christ? Three theological ideas dominate the contemporary religious discussion of salvation.

Universalism

Also known as pluralism, universalism teaches that there are many ways—or even an unlimited number of ways—to God and that everyone will eventually be saved and reach heaven. This is a popular position among liberal theologians, as well as among New Age adherents. This view is represented by liberal theologian John Hick, who says,

> Most New Testament scholars today do not believe that Jesus, the historical individual, claimed to be God incarnate. The old exclusivist view that only Christians are saved has been abandoned by the majority of Christian theologians and church leaders. There is, in fact, a basic moral outlook which is universal [in all religions], and I suggest that the concrete reality of salvation consists in embodying this in our lives in a spiritual transformation whose natural expression is unrestricted love and compassion. The basic moral teaching of the religions remains the same. It constitutes the universal ideal. What are called the conflicting truth-claims of the religions do not in fact conflict, because they are claims about different human awarenesses of the divine. We are living today in a time of transition which amounts to a move to a new paradigm of Christian thought.[29]

" 'God loved the world in this way: He gave His One and Only Son, so that everyone who believes in Him will not perish but have eternal life. God did not send His Son into the world that He might judge the world, but that the world might be saved through Him. Anyone who believes in Him is not judged, but anyone who does not believe is already judged, because he has not believed in the name of the One and Only Son of God' " (John 3:16-18).

Inclusivism

This view claims that Jesus is the only Savior but that it is possible for Jesus to save people even though they may never have personally trusted Him for salvation. Inclusivism teaches that people can receive salvation by responding to God's revelation in nature and conscience (called general revelation) or possibly even through other world religions. Although other religions have an imperfect understanding of the one true God, the truth they possess is believed to be adequate to save them. It is said that we may be able to recognize these "anonymous Christians," a phrase coined by the Roman Catholic theologian Karl Rahner, by their good deeds. Hence, belief in a works salvation often accompanies this position.

Clark Pinnock and John Sanders represent this perspective. Pinnock, for example, says:

> According to Acts 4:12, ... Jesus has done a unique work for the human race, the good news of which needs to be preached to the whole world. But this uniqueness does not entail exclusivity. ... The Son through whom all things were made is constantly at work in the world. The Spirit of God broods over the whole creation and over history. We should not think of God as absent from the world except where the name of Jesus of Nazareth is pronounced. Although for many evangelicals the finality of Christ spells exclusivism, I believe that our high Christology can also create space for openness and generosity to the world's peoples. We do not need to think of the church as the ark of salvation, leaving everyone else in hell. ... I have always been impressed by the view put forward at the Second Vatican Council to the effect that the person who dies having sincerely sought after God, but not having learned about Jesus, will not be automatically condemned in the judgment but will be given the opportunity to plead the blood of Christ.[30]

Sanders explains how he believes someone can get to heaven without personally trusting Christ: "The Father reaches out to the unevangelized through both the Son and the Spirit via general revelation, conscience and human culture. God does not leave himself without witness to any people. Salvation for the unevangelized is made possible only by the redemptive work of Jesus, but God applies that work even to those who are ignorant of the atonement. God does this if people respond in trusting faith to the revelation they have."[31]

" 'There is salvation in no one else, for there is no other name under heaven given to people by which we must be saved' " (Acts 4:12).

Exclusivism

Exclusivism is the teaching that the church has held for most of its history. This orthodox, evangelical position teaches that salvation comes only through a personal faith commitment to Jesus Christ as Savior and Lord. This requirement does not apply to those who die before reaching an age of moral responsibility and accountability, such as infants and small children, or to those who are incapable of moral discernment, such as mentally handicapped people. Baptists have generally held the view that these individuals are the objects of God's saving grace and mercy. But exclusivism affirms the absolute uniqueness and finality of God's revelation in Jesus. He alone is the Savior, the definitive and ultimate expression of divine truth. Only in Him can people be saved. God would not have sent His only Son to die on a cross if He could have saved us another way. The cross of Christ is God's greatest testimony that Jesus is the exclusive way to the Father.

> **"Christ is Christianity itself; He stands not outside of it but in its centre; without His name, person and work, there is no Christianity left. In a word, Christ does not point out the way to salvation; He is the Way itself."**[32]
> —*Benjamin B. Warfield*

Draw a line from each term to its correct description.

Exclusivism	**People can be saved by responding to God's revelation in nature and conscience or through other religions, even without trusting Christ.**
Universalism	**Salvation comes only through a personal faith commitment to Jesus Christ as Savior and Lord.**
Inclusivism	**There are many ways to God, and everyone will eventually be saved.**

How do Christians view the universalist and inclusivist claims of the religions we examined earlier? Proverbs 14:12 says,

> There is a way that seems right to a man,
> but in the end it leads to death.

Though they may differ in their particular teachings and rituals, all religions other than Christianity teach salvation by good works, self-reliance, or personal accomplishment. Only the gospel of Jesus Christ and His work on the cross proclaim the good news of salvation by grace through faith in the accomplishments of One who paid in full the price of sin as our Savior— Jesus, our Mediator.

Christians are often ridiculed and criticized for claiming that Jesus Christ is the only Savior for humankind. We are frequently called narrow-minded bigots. However, if we are to be true to our Lord and the Bible, we must proclaim such a message. This is exactly what Jesus said about Himself. In

John 14 our Lord spoke to the disciples the night before He was crucified. The disciples were troubled and discouraged by the news that Jesus would soon leave them. Furthermore, Jesus had revealed that He was going to die (see John 12:32-33), that one of the disciples would betray Him (see John 13:21), and that even Peter would deny Him three times (see John 13:37-38). Jesus sought to comfort the disciples with this promise and encouragement: " 'Your heart must not be troubled. Believe in God; believe also in Me' " (John 14:1).

Jesus then told the disciples that His departure was for a good reason (" 'to prepare a place for you,' " John 14:2) and that it was not permanent, because He would come back and take them to be with Him (see v. 3). Jesus said that they knew the way to the place He was going (see v. 4), but Thomas said he did not understand. His admission probably represented the thoughts of the other disciples as well. Jesus responded with one of the most important declarations in all of Scripture about the doctrine of salvation: " 'I am the way, the truth, and the life. No one comes to the Father except through Me' " (v. 6).

Note that verse 6 literally begins with the declaration "I Myself am the way." Jesus used an intensive pronoun to emphasize that He and He alone is the way, the truth, and the life. Significantly, the definite article *the* prominently appears before the words *way, truth,* and *life.* Contrary to popular opinions in the 21st century, salvation is not possible through many ways; there is only one way. As the way, Jesus is the path to God. He shows us how we can come to the Father. As the truth, Jesus is the presentation of God. He is the very embodiment of the revelation of God. As the life, Jesus is the power of God. He is able to breathe spiritual life into the souls of those who are spiritually dead (see Eph. 2:1-3).

Jesus reinforced this truth when He said, " 'No one comes to the Father except through Me' " (John 14:6). Jesus explained this staggering statement when He said that to know Him is to know the Father (see John 14:7). Whatever makes the Father God, Jesus is all of that as well. To know Jesus is to know God. To see Jesus is to see God (see John 14:9). When we come to Jesus, we can be sure we have come to the only true God.

Some inclusivists might argue that this particular text does not negate their argument. They might say, "Of course, Jesus is the only way to God, but that way may not require explicit faith in Him." However, the whole of John's Gospel is committed to the proposition that faith in Jesus is the means of salvation. D. A. Carson says, "The Gospel of John so repeatedly insists that faith in Jesus is the condition of salvation that the drift of this book is all in one direction."[34] Carson adds, "The Son's mission is never cast as providing eternal life for certain people whether they have believed in him or not."[35]

"Jesus said a totally exclusive word: 'No man cometh unto the Father but by me.' "[33]
—*Francis Schaeffer*

In Acts 4:8-12 Peter addressed the Sanhedrin. Filled with the Spirit (see v. 8), Peter boldly proclaimed the gospel of Jesus Christ and the salvation He has made available to the world. In verse 12 Peter made clear that only the name of Jesus will save: " 'There is salvation in no one else, for there is no other name under heaven given to people by which we must be saved' " (Acts 4:12). It is of great significance that Peter emphasized the name of Jesus. Such a declaration calls for a personal, conscious commitment to that name. John Polhill clearly states what is meant: "If there is salvation in no other name (v. 12), then obviously one must make a commitment to that sole name that brings salvation."[36] Nothing in the text or context indicates that this is possible for someone who has never heard the name of Jesus. Nor does this verse or any Scripture suggest that a postmortem opportunity will be made available. It was this understanding that drove the early church to evangelize the world. That same conviction should motivate us as well.

Read 1 Timothy 2:5-6. State every truth you find in these verses.

_____

_____

_____

What does the word *mediator* mean? _____

_____

Check your work as you study the following paragraphs.

"There is one God and one mediator between God and man, a man, Christ Jesus, who gave Himself— a ransom for all, a testimony at the proper time" (1 Tim. 2:5-6).

The apostle Paul also preached that Jesus is the only way to salvation. First Timothy was Paul's instruction manual to his son in the ministry, Timothy, about proper faith and practice in the church. Chapter 2 begins with specific principles of prayer for the people of God (see vv. 1-2). Paul then addressed the wonderful truth that God wants everyone to be saved and come to the knowledge of the truth (see v. 4). God's love is comprehensive and universal. No human being exists outside the reach of God's concern. Our God is a seeking God who is vitally concerned about the salvation of all (see 2 Pet. 3:9).

Although God has a universal interest in the souls of lost people, there is only one way a person can enter His presence: through the one mediator, the man Christ Jesus. Some scholars believe that 1 Timothy 2:5-6 is a partial fragment of a well-known confession of faith in the early church. Here Paul declared three undeniable truths of the Christian faith and the gospel message.

1. There is one God. Christianity is firmly rooted in the monotheism of the Hebrew faith and the Old Testament Scriptures. As the Shema of Deuteronomy 6:4 declares, "Hear, O Israel, the Lord [Yahweh] our God [Elohim], the Lord [Yahweh] is one."

2. There is only one way anyone can come to God: by the one mediator between God and people, Jesus Christ. Jesus' position as the one mediator between God and people excludes all others who claim to be able to bridge the gulf of sin that separates us from God. There is one way for us to approach God and come into His presence. We come only through the man who was also God in the flesh, Jesus Christ (see John 1:14).

3. Jesus gave "Himself—a ransom for all, a testimony at the proper time" (1 Tim. 2:5). Christ's work as the mediator satisfied our holy and righteous God (see Rom. 3:25) and reconciled humankind to God (see 2 Cor. 5:17-21). The basis for the Savior's work is His sacrificial, substitutionary death as a ransom for all. The word *ransom* means *to pay a price in order to obtain a release*. In Paul's day it carried the idea of paying the determined price in order to obtain the release of a slave. We were all slaves of sin, in bondage and shackled. We had no hope of ever setting ourselves free or being released. But in His great love for us (see Rom. 5:8; Eph. 2:4) Jesus Christ invaded our world and made the necessary payment to obtain our freedom from sin.

God's invitation is universal, but His salvation is particular, specific, and exclusive. It is only through His Son, Jesus. The eternal life that God gives is found only in Jesus and in no other (see 1 John 5:12). With confidence we can look into the face of anyone and say, "There is a God who made you and who loves you. Though you and I have sinned against Him and deserve the penalty of spiritual death and eternal separation from this God, He has made a way for all to enter His presence—through belief in His Son, Jesus."

Dr. W. H. Rogers was the pastor of First Baptist Church in New York City in the 1930s. In his book *The God-Man* he told the story of a woman who knew the Bible very well and could repeat many passages of Scripture from memory: "As the years rolled away her memory gradually weakened so that she could not recall much of which she had learned. One precious passage remained, 'I know whom I have believed and am persuaded that He is able to keep that which I have committed unto Him against that day.' Even that began to depart and she could only repeat, 'that which I have committed unto Him.' During the last few days the feebleness increased and as life ebbed away, she was heard repeating the last word, 'Him, Him, Him.'

"The one who has the Son has life. The one who doesn't have the Son of God does not have life" (1 John 5:12).

She had everything in that one word. The Living Word and the Life of the Written Word."[37]

The woman had it right. It's all about Jesus.

Suppose that a 10-year-old asks you, "Why did Jesus have to die?" Write your response to the child.

_____

_____

_____

_____

_____

"The wages of sin is death, but the gift of God is eternal life in Christ Jesus our Lord" (Rom. 6:23).

Assume that you have a neighbor who is not a Christian. You are good friends who freely talk about God and matters of faith. Respond to the following questions your neighbor asks.

"I was flipping channels Sunday and saw this preacher who was all wound up and going for it. He was amusing, so I stopped and watched him. He used a term I had never heard before—*total depravity.* He said that we are all totally depraved. That's nonsense! I'm not depraved! What did he mean by that term?"

_____

_____

_____

"He went on to talk about the atonement. What's that?"

_____

_____

_____

"Then he said that a person can come to God only through faith in Jesus Christ. No way! There are many ways to God, and what's true for one person may not be true for someone else. Why are you Christians so narrow-minded?"

_____

_____

_____

_____

_____

_____

Think of a friend or an acquaintance who is not a Christian. Write the person's name here.

_____

Commit to God that you will pray for this person every day. Ask Him to give you the opportunity to talk with this person about the meaning of Christ's death on the cross.

Spend time reflecting on this chapter. What was the most meaningful thing God showed you in your study?

_____

_____

_____

Close your study by singing the hymn in the margin as a prayer to God. If others hear you and ask why you are singing, tell them!

Answers to matching activity on page 86: 1. d, 2. a, 3. b, 4. e, 5. c

"When I survey
  the wondrous cross,
On which the Prince
  of glory died,
My richest gain
  I count but loss,
And pour contempt
  on all my pride.

See, from His head,
  His hands, His feet,
Sorrow and love flow
  mingled down;
Did e'er such love
  and sorrow meet,
Or thorns compose
  so rich a crown?

Were the whole realm
  of nature mine,
That were a present
  far too small;
Love so amazing, so divine,
Demands my soul, my life,
  my all."[38]

Chapter 5
Raised in Power and Glory

I have a friend named Mike who is not a Christian. In fact, he considers himself an atheist or agnostic, depending on which day it is. Mike is incredibly intelligent. He is also quite curious. That curiosity led Mike to Criswell College in Dallas, Texas, around 1990 to live in an evangelical community and write about his experience. Surprisingly, especially to his editors, Mike did not produce the hatchet job they expected. He was actually quite complimentary about what he found.

After spending almost six months with us going to classes; attending a pastor's conference in Jacksonville, Florida; traveling on a mission trip; and observing a Southern Baptist Convention annual meeting, it was time for Mike to return to his home in New York City. My wife and our four sons had become fond of Mike, so we invited him over for dinner before he left. As we were talking after dinner, I asked Mike, "After all you have studied and experienced, what is the bottom line, as you see it?"

With no hesitation Mike responded, "That's easy. It's Jesus' resurrection from the dead." Mike then set forth the logic of the issue: "If Jesus rose from the dead, then there is a God, and Jesus is that God. Furthermore, the Bible is true because He said it is true and believed it is true. That means heaven and hell are real, and your relationship with Jesus determines which way you go." I have often wished my seminary students and fellow theologians saw the issue as clearly as this agnostic/atheist.

Christianity stands or falls with the bodily resurrection of Jesus. It really is that simple. The apostle Paul certainly understood it that way. Read these verses from his great resurrection chapter, 1 Corinthians 15: "If Christ has not been raised, then our preaching is without foundation, and so is your faith. In addition, we are found to be false witnesses about God, because we have testified about God that He raised up Christ—whom He did not raise up. And if Christ has not been raised, your faith is worthless; you are still in your sins" (vv. 14-15,17).

Paul's argument is plain and concise, as Thiessen shows: "It [the resurrection] is the fundamental doctrine of Christianity. Many admit the necessity of the death of Christ who deny the importance of the bodily resurrection of Christ. But that Christ's physical resurrection is vitally important is evident from the fundamental connection of this doctrine with Christianity.

Chapter 5 Learning Goals
- **You will be able to summarize historical facts affirming Jesus' bodily resurrection.**
- **You will be able to share your personal experience that affirms Jesus' resurrection.**
- **You will be able to face adversity with hope and assurance because of Jesus' resurrection.**

Ask God to speak to your heart as you study this chapter.

"The resurrection of Jesus is the keystone to the arch of Christianity. It is the seal of all His claims to the Messiahship and Divine Sonship. Without the resurrection, He could not be the Saviour of mankind."[1]
—*J. W. Shepard*

In 1 Cor. 15:12-19 Paul shows that everything stands or falls with Christ's bodily resurrection: apostolic preaching is vain (v. 14), the apostles are false witnesses (v. 15), the Corinthians are yet in their sins (v. 17), those fallen asleep in Christ have perished (v. 18), and Christians are of all men most miserable (v. 19), if Christ has not risen."[2]

It is difficult, if not impossible, to explain the birth of the church and its gospel message apart from Jesus' resurrection. The whole of New Testament faith and teaching orbits around the confession and conviction that the crucified Jesus is the Son of God, established and vindicated as such "by the resurrection from the dead according to the Spirit of holiness" (Rom. 1:4). William Lane Craig notes the relevance of the resurrection now and for the future: "Against the dark background of modern man's despair, the Christian proclamation of the resurrection is a bright light of hope. The earliest Christians saw Jesus' resurrection as both the vindication of His personal claims and as a harbinger of our own resurrection to eternal life. If Jesus rose from the dead, then His claims are vindicated and our Christian hope is sure; if Jesus did not rise, our faith is futile and we fall back into despair."[3]

The Resurrection Under Attack

Skeptics from outside the church have attacked the bodily resurrection from the very beginning. However, the fact that people who claim to be Christians have launched attacks against the truth of Jesus' bodily resurrection is baffling. Schubert Ogden, of the Perkins School of Theology on the campus of Southern Methodist University, dismisses Jesus' bodily resurrection as both impossible and irrelevant: "If per impossible, the corpse of a man was actually resuscitated, this would be just as relevant to my salvation as an existing self or person as that the carpenter next door just drove a nail in a two-by-four, or that American technicians have at last been successful in recovering a nose cone that had been first placed in orbit around the earth."[4]

On April 10, 1998, the infamous Jesus Seminar released its second major work, *The Acts of Jesus: The Search for the Authentic Deeds of Jesus.* A prepress release boldly proclaimed:

Jesus According to THE ACTS OF JESUS:
Jesus was not born of a virgin; Jesus' father was either Joseph or some unknown male who either seduced or raped the young Mary.

Jesus was an itinerant sage and a social deviant. Wandering about from place to place, teaching and healing and living on handouts—he regularly infringed the social codes in force in his society.

Jesus was considered a healer during his lifetime. From today's perspective, Jesus' cures are related to psychosomatic maladies.

Jesus did not walk on water, feed the multitudes with loaves and fishes, change water into wine, or raise Lazarus from the dead.

The body of Jesus probably decayed as do all corpses. The resurrection of Jesus was not something that happened on the first Easter Sunday; it was not an event that could have been captured by a video camera.[5]

Also, in spring 1998 Bill Phipps, the elected moderator of the United Church of Canada, said, "I don't believe Jesus was God, but I'm no theologian. I don't believe Jesus is the only way to God. I don't believe he rose from the dead as scientific fact. I don't know whether these things happened. It's an irrelevant question."[6]

These recent attacks on the bodily resurrection of Jesus are not new. Rooted in the Enlightenment, they exalt rationalism and spring from an antisupernatural worldview. The German scholar Rudolf Bultmann (1884–1976) set the tone for this understanding of the New Testament around 1950. *The Myth of God Incarnate* (1977) attempted to mythologize the entire Christ event. The Jesus Seminar and their fellows are basically attempting to put new life into Bultmann's work.

When we approach the issue of Jesus' bodily resurrection, we are confronted with three basic options.

Option 1: Jesus' resurrection is false—a great hoax. This position holds that Jesus did not rise from the dead and that certain persons, probably the disciples, fabricated a lie and pulled off one of the best hoaxes, if not the greatest hoax, of all time.

Option 2: Jesus' resurrection is fiction—nice mythology. In this view, the early church made Jesus into someone and something He really was not by telling stories about Him that they embellished more and more over time. Eventually, believers turned Him into God incarnate, who died on a cross for our sins and later rose from the dead. This option asserts that although none of these events really happened, the stories about Jesus continue to evoke wonder and inspire us to live more noble lives.

Option 3: Jesus' resurrection is fact—the supreme event of history. This view argues that the New Testament accurately records the historical and supernatural resurrection of Jesus of Nazareth from the dead. His resurrection was bodily and permanent. Further, various witnesses saw the resurrected Christ on numerous occasions and testified, some even to the point of martyrdom, to the reality of the resurrection.

> **"Without belief in the resurrection of Jesus, Christianity doesn't make sense."[7]**
> —*William L. Hendricks*

Those of us who affirm the truth of option 3 bear the burden of proof. After all, we claim that Jesus did what no other person has ever done: He died, rose from the dead, and remains alive today. Before constructing a defense for the historical, evangelical position of Jesus' bodily resurrection, we will examine the philosophies behind options 1 and 2.

Naturalistic Theories That Reject the Resurrection

Naturalistic theories attempt to explain away the idea that Jesus was bodily resurrected by the supernatural power of God. These theories prefer any naturalistic explanation of the event over a supernatural one. Naturalistic ideas were popularized by 19th-century liberal theologians, and some of them are still prevalent today. Following is a brief survey of these theories.

The swoon theory. This view argues that Jesus did not really die but fainted because of the enormous physical punishment He suffered. Later regaining consciousness in the cool, damp tomb, He unwrapped Himself and got out of His grave clothes. He then managed to move aside the large stone that sealed the entrance to the tomb. Bruised, bleeding, battered, and beaten, Jesus emerged from the tomb and convinced His followers that He had risen from the dead.

Some variations exist within this view. In his best-seller *The Passover Plot* Hugh Schonfield says Jesus planned the whole thing with help from Joseph of Arimathea. Jesus was drugged while on the cross, making it appear that He had died. Unfortunately, He was seriously injured and actually died a short time later.[9] An outrageous expression of this view is that of Barbara Thiering, who teaches at the University of Sydney, Australia. She believes that Jesus was crucified alongside Judas and Simon Magus at Qumran. He was given snake poison to fake His death and later recovered. He would go on to marry Mary Magdalene and later Lydia, and He would father several children![10]

The spirit theory. According to this view, Jesus was not raised bodily, but He returned in a spirit form or as a spirit creature. This view is sometimes popular among liberal theologians who have mystical interests, as well as among New Age followers. Another group that holds this view is the Jehovah's Witnesses cult, which teaches that Jesus was created by God as the archangel Michael and that while on earth He was only a man. Following His death on the cross, God restored Jesus in a spiritual form only. The Watchtower Society asserts, "King Christ Jesus was put to death in the flesh and was resurrected an invisible spirit creature."[11] In fact, Jehovah's Witnesses believe Jesus' physical return to heaven would have been humili-

> "The early Christians did not believe that Jesus was risen again because they could not find his dead body. They believed because they had found the living Christ. When they first began to proclaim Jesus in public as the risen Lord, they did not say, 'We found his tomb empty,' but 'We saw him alive.' "[8]
> —*F. F. Bruce*

ating: "Jesus did not take his human body to heaven to be forever a man in heaven. Had he done so, that would have left him even lower than the angels. … God did not purpose for Jesus to be humiliated thus forever by being a fleshly man forever. No, but after he had sacrificed his perfect manhood, God raised him to deathless life as a glorious spirit creature."[12]

The hallucination theory. The German scholar David Strauss (1808–74) originally set forth this perspective. How do you explain the alleged appearances of Jesus to His disciples? He argued, "According to our view the imagination of his [Jesus'] followers aroused in their deepest spirit, presented their master revived, for they could not possibly think of him as dead. What for a long time was valid as an external fact, first miraculous, then deceptive, finally simply natural, is hereby reduced completely to the state of mind and made into an inner event."[13]

A creative modern version of this idea was proposed by Ian Wilson, who believes that Jesus preprogrammed His disciples to hallucinate by means of hypnosis. He says, "It is possible that he [Jesus] prepared his disciples for his resurrection using the technique that modern hypnotists call post-hypnotic suggestion. By this means he could have effectively conditioned them to hallucinate his appearances in response to certain prearranged cues (the breaking of bread?), for a predetermined period after his death."[14]

The vision theory. This theory asserts that the disciples had experiences they interpreted or understood to be literal appearances of the risen Jesus. For example, Jürgen Moltmann believes that the disciples saw visionary appearances of the risen Christ and that He communicated to them a call and mission.[15] Though not identical, this view is similar to the spirit theory.

The legend/myth theory. Basically the view of the Jesus Seminar, this theory holds that over time the Jesus stories were embellished and exaggerated. Some in this camp even deny that the historical Jesus of Nazareth existed, though their numbers are quite small. Radically committed to an antisupernatural agenda, proponents of this view separate the Jesus of history (who He really was) from the Christ of faith (what the church later imagined Him to be). They see the resurrection as a wonder story indicating the significance the mythical Jesus held for His followers. The tomb, this position claims, most certainly was not empty.

The stolen-body theory. This is the earliest theory that attempts to explain away Jesus' bodily resurrection. It goes back to Matthew 28:11-15, which records that the soldiers who guarded Jesus' tomb were bribed by the Jewish leaders to lie and say, " ' "His disciples came during the night and stole Him while we were sleeping" ' " (v. 13). Occasionally, it is alleged that the body could also have been stolen by the Jewish leaders, the Romans, or even

"Some of the guard came into the city and reported to the chief priests everything that had happened. After the priests had assembled with the elders and agreed on a plan, they gave the soldiers a large sum of money and told them, 'Say this, "His disciples came during the night and stole Him while we were sleeping." If this reaches the governor's ears, we will deal with him and keep you out of trouble.' So they took the money and did as they were instructed. And this story has been spread among Jewish people to this day" (Matt. 28:11-15).

Joseph of Arimathea. Deists in the 18th century briefly revived this theory, but virtually no one holds it today.[16]

The wrong-tomb theory. This theory asserts that belief in Jesus' bodily resurrection rests on a simple mistake: first the women and later the men went to the wrong tomb by accident. Finding the wrong tomb empty, they erroneously concluded that Jesus had risen from the dead. A liberal theologian named Kirsopp Lake first defended this theory in 1907, but it attracted almost no followers.

The lie-for-profit theory. Some have claimed that Jesus' alleged resurrection was perhaps the greatest religious hoax ever attempted and was perpetrated by His disciples. Jesus' death by crucifixion was a huge disappointment, but His followers saw a way to turn it for good and financial profit. They proclaimed that Jesus had risen, built a substantial following, and profited from the monies they fleeced from people. You will be hard pressed to find this theory in any book, though I have heard cynical skeptics express it from time to time. Further, if this was indeed the apostles' plan, it was a colossal failure, because all Jesus' disciples except John died as martyrs.

The mistaken-identity theory. Sometimes related to the wrong-tomb theory, this view says the women mistook someone for Jesus. They perhaps ran into a gardener or a caretaker in the garden. Because it was early in the morning, it was dark, and they could not clearly see this man. He may have been standing or working near an empty tomb, the wrong tomb. When he informed them that Jesus was not in there, they mistakenly drew the conclusion that He had risen. Supporters of this view sometimes refer to John 20:11-18. There Mary Magdalene initially did not recognize Jesus, and the text says she supposed "He was the gardener" (see v. 15). However, she quickly discovered it was Jesus and got a close look. Verse 17 says that Jesus had to tell her to let go of Him. At such close range she would not have mistaken another man for Jesus.

The twin theory. In a 1995 debate with Christian apologist William Lane Craig, philosopher Robert Greg Cavin argued that Jesus had an identical twin brother. Separated at birth, they did not see each other again until the crucifixion. Following Jesus' death, His twin conjured up a messianic identity and mission for Jesus, stole His body, and pretended to be the risen Jesus. Craig rightly notes that imaginative theories like Cavin's are humorous, but they have no value for those who seriously want to discover what really happened on the first Easter morning.[17]

" 'Don't cling to Me,' Jesus told her, 'for I have not yet ascended to the Father' " (John 20:17).

Read Matthew 28:1-10 and Mark 16:1-11. Write the way Mary Magdalene might have responded to the previous theories.

_____

_____

Read 1 Corinthians 15:1-24. Write the way Paul might have responded to the same false theories.

_____

_____

" 'I know you are looking for Jesus who was crucified. He is not here! For He has been resurrected, just as He said. Come and see the place where He lay' " (Matt. 28:5-6).

The Muslim theory. Islam rejects the biblical witness of Jesus' crucifixion, teaching instead that God provided a substitute for Jesus, perhaps even making the person look like Jesus. Surah 4:157 in the Qur'an says, "They declared: 'We have put to death the Messiah Jesus the son of Mary, the apostle of Allah.' They did not kill him, nor did they crucify him, but they thought they did."[18] Muslims do not agree on who took Jesus' place. Candidates include Judas, Pilate, Simon of Cyrene, or even one of the disciples.[19] Muslims do not believe in Jesus' bodily resurrection because they do not believe He died on the cross. Instead, Surah 4:158 declares, "Allah took him up into Himself."

Islam teaches that Jesus was a prophet of God, was born of a virgin, and performed miracles. However, the Muslim faith is inadequate and erroneous in its view of who Jesus is and what He came to do. Below are Islamic beliefs about Jesus and denials of Him. Record a Scripture reference that refutes each false belief.

Muslim Teaching	Scripture Reference
Jesus was a mere human being, superseded by Muhammad.	_____
Jesus was not God.	_____
Jesus is not the unique, divine Son of God.	_____
Jesus did not die on the cross.	_____
Jesus was not bodily resurrected.	_____
Salvation is not through Christ.	_____

"The Pharisees couldn't
stand Him but found
they couldn't stop Him.
Satan tried to tempt Him
but found he couldn't
trip Him.
[Pilate] examined Him
on trial but found he
couldn't fault Him.
The Romans crucified
Him but found they
couldn't take His life.
Death couldn't handle
Him, and the grave
couldn't hold Him."[20]
— *Anne Graham Lotz*

Contemporary Views
of the Resurrection

Scholars today, especially liberal biblical scholars and theologians, operate from a naturalistic worldview. They reject God's supernatural activity in the world, and this bias colors all of their conclusions. In addition, they hold to an existential/experiential understanding of faith and religion. That is, what counts for them in matters of faith is experience or feeling—someone's personal, subjective response—rather than an informed commitment to the truth of God and His Word.

The naturalistic theories of the 19th century basically devoured one another, so that they are seldom held today as they once were.[21] They were found to be flawed and wanting, so scholars moved on. But where? After all, if you are committed to antisupernaturalism, and you rule out the possibility of Jesus' supernatural, bodily resurrection, what do you do? You develop more sophisticated theories that often prove vague and unclear. We can summarize recent thinking on the bodily resurrection in terms of five models.

The resurrection appearances are dismissed or seriously questioned. These scholars dismiss literal claims that Jesus' tomb was empty or that His followers actually saw Him. They conclude that the nature of the original eyewitnesses' experiences cannot be discovered.

The resurrection is literally true but cannot be historically verified. These scholars assert that the resurrection can be accepted only by faith. Karl Barth, for example, believed that the resurrection should be accepted by faith as a literal event but that it cannot be established by historical investigation.

The resurrection is probable. These scholars set forth an abstract reconstruction of the historical nature of Jesus' appearances. Often providing reasons that the empty tomb is the best explanation for all of the data, they seek "to ascertain at least a minimalistic understanding of what really happened, including the providing of reasons for the acceptance of the appearances of Jesus and the empty tomb."[22] However, they hold that the resurrection cannot be demonstrated by historical methodology. Jesus' appearances are usually viewed as spiritual in nature rather than a physical phenomenon.

Available historical data demonstrate the probability that the tomb was empty and that Jesus was literally raised from the dead. Pannenberg thinks the historical facts support the likelihood of the empty tomb and Jesus' literal appearances. However, he conceives of Jesus' appearances in terms of a spiritual body that appeared from heaven; was recognized as Jesus when He spoke; and, at least in Paul's case, was accompanied by a phenomenon of light.

The tomb in which Jesus was buried was found empty, and Jesus actually appeared to His followers. This model, the historic, orthodox position, holds that the evidence refutes the naturalistic theories. The major difference between this model and the previous one is that scholars in this group believe that Jesus rose bodily. Jesus rose from the dead in the same body in which He was crucified, though it was a transformed resurrection kind of body (see 1 Cor. 15:35-49). Scholars who hold this view are usually evangelicals.[23]

An Affirmation of Jesus' Bodily Resurrection

Why should anyone believe in the bodily resurrection of Jesus of Nazareth? Isn't the claim simply unbelievable? Christians make a one-of-a-kind claim for an event that has never been duplicated at any time in any place by any other person. We must bear the burden of proof, and the evidence must be strong. Let's gather all the data and examine what is revealed.

Scholars acknowledge a number of historical facts surrounding Jesus' death, burial, and resurrection.

1. Jesus died on a Roman cross by crucifixion.
2. Jesus was buried in a tomb not far from the crucifixion site.
3. Jesus' death threw the disciples into a state of despair and despondency, believing that their Lord was now dead.
4. Jesus' tomb was discovered to be empty shortly after His burial.
5. The disciples had real and genuine experiences that convinced them beyond a shadow of a doubt that Jesus had risen from the dead and that He was alive.
6. These experiences with the risen Jesus radically transformed the disciples into bold witnesses of His resurrection from the dead, a witness that led to martyrdom for many of them.
7. The message of Jesus' death, burial, and resurrection was the heart of the gospel from the beginning of the church's existence.
8. This gospel was preached in Jerusalem, the very city where Jesus had been crucified and buried.
9. The good news of Christ's death and resurrection was foundational in the birth of the Christian church.
10. Sunday, not the Sabbath, became the day of worship for the church in celebration of the Lord's resurrection on that day.
11. James, Jesus' half-brother and an unbeliever, was converted following an appearance of his resurrected brother.
12. Saul, a persecutor of Christians, was converted to Christianity following an appearance of the risen Christ.

The good news of Christ's death and resurrection was foundational in the birth of the Christian church.

Any theory or explanation of the empty tomb must properly account for all of these facts to be compelling and credible. It is interesting to note that no one witnessed the actual resurrection of Jesus. In fact, the Gospels make no such claim. The belief and proclamation of Jesus' resurrection are based on the fact that He died, He was buried, the tomb in which He was buried was discovered to be empty, and the disciples had experiences that convinced them that Jesus had supernaturally and bodily risen from the dead.[25]

Having established these historical facts, we can build a case for Jesus' bodily resurrection. Evidence can be divided into the following two categories.

Subjective Evidence

Subjective evidence, sometimes called the pragmatic test, is the evidence of experience. It asks these questions: Does an encounter with Jesus change lives? Does He make a difference in my life? Do Christ and Christianity work?

Subjective evidence includes the testimony of personal experience. Perhaps no line of evidence is more powerful than this when it comes to sharing your faith. Describing your life before you met Jesus, the way you received Him as Savior and Lord, and the difference He has made in your life is a powerful witnessing tool. However, we must acknowledge that other religions also claim to have religious experiences. Buddhists, Hindus, Muslims, Jews, New Agers, and others often claim to have had experiences that changed their lives. Therefore, experience in and of itself is not sufficient to make the case for Jesus' resurrection.

Objective Evidence

We must add to our defense objective evidence. We cannot prove the bodily resurrection of Jesus through a scientific formula or experiment. In fact, we cannot prove anything in history this way. When we speak of objective evidence, we mean historically verifiable evidence. Our model is a courtroom, where witnesses are called and a judgment is rendered. The question to answer is this: Does the evidence persuade us that we have good reason to believe that this alleged event really happened?

> One biblical scholar said that the three living proofs of Christ's resurrection are the church, the New Testament, and Sunday as a day of worship.[26] State how each of these substantiates the resurrection.
>
> The church: _____
>
> _____

"Meeting Jesus Christ is the single most important event of any and every life."[24]
—*Robert Rasmussen*

106

The New Testament: _____

_____

Sunday as a day of worship: _____

_____

Check your work as you read the next section.

I believe we can marshal a strong case of compelling evidence that Christ indeed rose from the dead.

The failure of naturalistic theories to explain the event. As we noted, the naturalistic arguments of the previous centuries did not stand up to careful analysis. Virtually all of them have been abandoned or substantially revised, and even liberal scholars seldom embrace them today. Proponents were selective in the biblical data they affirmed, accepting whatever helped their theories and rejecting whatever did not.

The birth of the disciples' faith and the radical change in their lives. Something happened that caused Jesus' followers to believe that they had genuine encounters with the risen Lord. Furthermore, these encounters with Jesus changed them from fearful cowards in hiding to bold witnesses of the resurrected Christ. In addition, according to church tradition, each disciple, with the exception of John, died as a martyr. Each died alone, and yet each one died still proclaiming Jesus as the risen Lord with their dying breath. The importance of this observation can scarcely be overstated. Although people will die for a lie, thinking it is the truth, they will not die for what they know is a lie. In an interview with Lee Strobel, the Christian philosopher J. P. Moreland said this about the disciples:

> They were willing to spend the rest of their lives proclaiming this [Jesus' resurrection], without any payoff from a human point of view. It's not as though there were a mansion awaiting them on the Mediterranean. They faced a life of hardship. They often went without food, slept exposed to the elements, were ridiculed, beaten, imprisoned. And finally, most of them were executed in torturous ways. For what? For good intentions? No, because they were convinced beyond a shadow of a doubt that they had seen Jesus Christ alive from the dead. What you can't explain is how this particular group of men came up with this particular belief without having had an experience of the resurrected Christ. There's no other adequate explanation.[27]

"The only way the complete transformation in the disciples can be accounted for, as well as their success in preaching the resurrection in the very place where their Master had been crucified, is to take the Gospel records seriously in what they tell us about the empty tomb and the appearances."[28]
—*Everett F. Harrison*

Strobel, a former skeptic and agnostic, adds, "The disciples were in a position to know without a doubt whether or not Jesus had risen from the dead. ... If they weren't absolutely certain, they wouldn't have allowed themselves to be tortured to death for proclaiming that the Resurrection had happened."[29]

Even the Jewish scholar Pinchas Lapide sees the force of this argument. Though he is not a Christian, he surprisingly believes that Jesus rose from the dead. Why? I will let him speak for himself: "The resurrection of Jesus was a real historical occurrence, and not something first and foremost taking place in the hearts and minds of the first believers. The crucifixion of Jesus by itself could not have motivated the courage of martyrdom and unquenchable hope for the cause of salvation which Jesus preached and embodied in his actions."[30]

The empty tomb and the discarded grave clothes. The Christian movement could have been quickly crushed by producing Jesus' dead corpse. Evidently, no one was able to do so. William Lane Craig points to evidence supporting the fact that Jesus' tomb was empty:

- The historical reliability of the account of Jesus' burial supports the empty tomb.
- Paul's early testimony in 1 Corinthians 15 supports the truth of the empty tomb.
- The empty-tomb account is part of Mark's source material and is old, perhaps dating to within seven years of Jesus' crucifixion.
- The phrase "the first day of the week" is very ancient.
- The account itself is simple and lacks legendary development.
- The tomb was probably discovered empty by women.
- The disciples could not have preached the resurrection in Jerusalem had the tomb not been empty.
- The earliest Jewish propaganda against the Christians presupposes the empty tomb.[31]

To Craig's impressive list I would add that the grave clothes left behind make the case nearly irrefutable (see John 20:3-5). First, this detail is theologically and historically insignificant. The only reason to mention it is the fact that Peter and John saw them. Second, grave robbers do not unwrap a body they steal from a tomb! They grab the body and run. The most compelling reason the grave clothes were left behind is that the One who had been in them no longer needed them!

The fact that women saw the empty tomb first. In the Jewish culture of the first century, women were not qualified to be witnesses in a legal proceeding. Deemed unreliable, they could not testify in a court of law. Given this fact, it is astonishing that the Bible records that women saw the

"Peter and the other disciple went out, heading for the tomb. The two were running together, but the other disciple outran Peter and got to the tomb first. Stooping down, he saw the linen cloths lying there" (John 20:3-5).

risen Jesus first. If the early church was trying to persuade people to believe that Jesus rose from the dead, saying that women saw Him first was not a wise strategy. If the account of the empty tomb was fictional, it is also inconceivable that women would be the first witnesses to the event. The only reason to record that women saw Him first is that women saw Him first.[32]

The change in the day of worship from the Sabbath to Sunday. For centuries Jewish identity has been connected to the observance of the Sabbath, a day that is honored and kept sacred to the Lord. Yet something extraordinary happened around A.D. 30 that caused a large group of Jews in Jerusalem to change their day of worship from the Sabbath to Sunday: the bodily resurrection of Jesus from the dead. Robert Stein points to the antiquity of this change and its connection to the empty tomb: "The only tradition involving the first day of the week is the tradition of the empty tomb. ... The fact that the switch from Sabbath to Sunday took place early in the life of the church indicates that the tradition of the empty tomb was known from the beginning."[33]

The unlikely nature of mass hallucination. Mass hallucination is not only unlikely but also impossible. Hallucinations are inner, subjective experiences of the mind. They occur personally and individually, not as a group experience. Jesus' repeated appearances at different times and to different people are a death knell to this explanation.

Postresurrection appearances. The New Testament records several occasions when Jesus appeared to His followers shortly following His resurrection. Thirteen distinct appearances stand out.

> Read the following references to Jesus' postresurrection appearances and indicate the person(s) who witnessed each appearance. Also indicate other evidence of Jesus' resurrection, if given. The first one is completed for you as an example.

Reference	Witness(es)	Other Evidence
Matthew 28:1-10	Mary Magdalene, the other Mary	Stone rolled back; angel's appearance
Matthew 28:16-20; Mark 16:14-18	_____ _____	_____ _____
Luke 24:13-35	_____ _____	_____ _____

"Mary Magdalene went and announced to the disciples, 'I have seen the Lord!' " (John 20:18).

Luke 24:34;
1 Corinthians 15:5   _____   _____
                          _____   _____

Luke 24:36-49;
John 20:19-25   _____   _____
                          _____   _____

John 20:11-18   _____   _____
                          _____   _____
                          _____   _____

"He appeared to Cephas,
   then to the Twelve.   John 20:24-31   _____   _____
Then He appeared   _____   _____
   to over 500 brothers
   at one time. ...   John 21   _____   _____
Then He appeared   _____   _____
   to James, then to
   all the apostles.   Acts 1:4-9   _____   _____
Last of all, as to one   _____   _____
   abnormally born,
   He also appeared to me" Acts 9:1-9;
(1 Cor. 15:5-8).   1 Corinthians 15:8   _____   _____
                                                _____   _____

                           1 Corinthians 15:6   _____   _____
                                                _____   _____

                           1 Corinthians 15:7   _____   _____
                                                _____   _____

                           Revelation 1:9-18   _____   _____
                                                _____   _____

We can make several important observations about these appearances.
> • The disciples claimed that Jesus appeared at different times and
>   to different people.
> • Some appearances were to groups, while others were to individuals.
> • The differing though complementary natures of the resurrection
>   appearances support their authenticity. Harmonizing the resurrection

appearances is not easy. Stein even points out that "many scholars have despaired of ever arriving at a satisfactory solution."[34] This fact provides evidence that Jesus' followers did not meet together to concoct and agree on a story.

- The appearances lasted for 40 days and then came to a complete and abrupt stop. Acts 1:4-11 tells us why: Jesus' ascension back to heaven. No other compelling alternative explanation exists.

The 50-day interval between the resurrection and the proclamation of the gospel at Pentecost in Jerusalem. Jesus' disciples did not proclaim the gospel of the risen Lord for 50 days after the event took place. Why? What would explain this delay in public witness when delay could only hurt the cause, especially if they were planning to proclaim a hoax? Again the biblical witness is clear and compelling. They waited until Jesus had ascended (see Luke 24; Acts 1) and until the Holy Spirit had come to empower them for witness (see Acts 2). Christ had to leave before they would act on their own, and the Spirit had to come to give them boldness for witness.

The inability of the Jewish leaders and the Romans to disprove the message of the empty tomb. It is an undeniable fact of history that those who opposed and crucified Jesus could not disprove His resurrection. The earliest attempt to explain the empty tomb was to say the disciples had stolen the body (see Matt. 28:11-15). It is significant that even in the beginning the rulers did not deny that the tomb was empty. As previously noted, all they had to do was produce the body of Jesus to put an end to the Christian movement. Again, it appears there was no body to produce.

The unexpected nature of Jesus' bodily resurrection. The disciples did not anticipate that Jesus would rise from the dead, though He had predicted this miracle on several occasions (see Mark 8:31-33; 9:31-32; 10:32-34). In fact, Mark 9:32 tells us they did not understand. Perhaps they thought He was again speaking in parables. When Jesus was crucified, their hopes were dashed. They, like the two on the road to Emmaus, "were hoping that He was the One who was about to redeem Israel" (Luke 24:21). They looked for and hoped for a mighty Messiah who would deliver them from Roman oppression and restore the glory of Israel, as in the days of King David. A dying and rising Messiah was not what they expected, in spite of the fact that the Old Testament clearly predicted Him. The fact that the disciples were fearful, despondent, and in despair is especially fatal to any type of hallucination or hypnosis theory. All the evidence strongly affirms that the disciples did not anticipate Jesus' resurrection. Therefore, they could not have played a role in making it appear that He had risen.

The conversion of two skeptics. John 7:5 makes clear that James, the half-

"He was teaching His disciples and telling them, 'The Son of Man is being betrayed into the hands of men. They will kill Him, and after He is killed, He will rise three days later.' But they did not understand this statement, and they were afraid to ask Him" (Mark 9:31-32).

brother of Jesus, was an unbeliever in Jesus as Messiah prior to His crucifixion. Yet something happened that transformed James from a doubter to a believer, from a skeptic to a leader in the church at Jerusalem, from one who thought his brother was mad (see Mark 3:21) to one who willingly suffered martyrdom for the gospel. James was killed in A.D. 62 for his faith in Jesus as the risen Christ. Something remarkable occurred that brought about this radical change in James.

> Read Mark 3:21; John 7:5 (use several translations); and 1 Corinthians 15:7. Most likely, James was converted at Jesus' postresurrection appearance recorded in 1 Corinthians 15:7. What part do you think Jesus' resurrection played in James's conversion?

_____

_____

Saul of Tarsus violently persecuted the church (see Acts 7:58; 8:1-3; 9:1-2). However, something happened in Saul's life that changed him from a persecutor of Christ to a missionary and evangelist for Christ. His own testimony, recorded several times in Scripture, affirms that he saw the resurrected Christ (see Acts 9:3-6; 22:6-10; 26:12-19; 1 Cor. 15:8; Gal. 1:15-16). Saul was not open to the gospel. It took the resurrected Lord to convince him that Jesus was indeed the Christ.

"As [Saul] traveled and was nearing Damascus, a light from heaven suddenly flashed around him. Falling to the ground, he heard a voice saying to him, 'Saul, Saul, why are you persecuting Me?' 'Who are You, Lord?' he said. 'I am Jesus, whom you are persecuting,' He replied" (Acts 9:3-6).

> Read Acts 7:54-60; 8:1-3; 9:1-9. These verses describe Saul's life before he met the risen Lord on the Damascus road. What part do you think Jesus' resurrection played in Saul's conversion?

_____

_____

The moral character of the eyewitnesses. The New Testament provides the greatest teachings found in any literature on love, truth, honesty, hope, faithfulness, kindness—and the list goes on. These teachings came from the pens of men like Matthew, John, Paul, James, and Peter, all of whom claimed to be eyewitnesses of the risen Jesus. To affirm their teachings and yet reject their witness to Jesus as a lie or mistake is illogical and nonsensical. If we accept their teachings, we must trust their testimony about Jesus.

The early creedal witness of 1 Corinthians 15:3-8. The resurrection was the heart of the earliest Christian teaching, as shown in 1 Corinthians 15:3-8. Virtually all scholars agree that Paul recorded there a very early creed about Jesus' death and resurrection, a creed that predates Paul's letter. Habermas notes, "That this material is traditional and earlier than Paul is evident from numerous considerations, such as the usage of the technical terms 'delivered' and 'received' (which indicate the imparting of oral tradition), the parallelism and somewhat stylized content, the proper names of Peter and James. … Further pointers to the presence of traditional material include the Aramaic name Cephas (see the parallel in Luke 24:34), … and the two references to the fulfillment of the Scriptures."[35]

Some scholars even date Paul's receiving of this creed within a decade of the crucifixion itself, or from about A.D. 30–40. Most think that Paul probably heard this testimony during his visit in Jerusalem with Peter and James, who are included in the list of resurrection appearances (see 1 Cor. 15:5,7; Gal. 1:18-19).

How did Bible scholars come to this conclusion? First, all scholars agree that Paul wrote 1 Corinthians in A.D. 55–57. Second, Paul indicated in 1 Corinthians 15:3 that what he was about to write was what he preached when he evangelized them on his second missionary journey (see Acts 18:1-17). The second missionary journey dates to A.D. 50–52. But remember, Paul already possessed this crucifixion-resurrection creedal formula before he went to Corinth. Based on Galatians 1:13-22, Paul possessed this possibly as early as his conversion near Damascus or his visit to Jerusalem, bringing us up to A.D. 30–40.

This reconstruction of the events undermines any type of mythical or fable embellishment. First, there was not enough time for such embellishment to occur. Second, eyewitnesses could provide a check and balance to any inaccurate or exaggerated claims. It is clear that from the very beginning of Christianity, Jesus' bodily resurrection was at the center of the faith.

> Read 1 Corinthians 15:12-19. If Jesus' resurrection is not a historical truth, what are some of the results or consequences for us and our Christian faith, according to this passage?

_____

_____

_____

> "… that Christ died
> for our sins according
> to the Scriptures,
> that He was buried,
> that He was raised on
> the third day according
> to the Scriptures,
> and that He appeared
> to Cephas, then
> to the Twelve.
> Then He appeared
> to over 500 brothers
> at one time,
> most of whom remain
> to the present, but some
> have fallen asleep.
> Then He appeared
> to James, then to
> all the apostles.
> Last of all, as to one
> abnormally born,
> He also appeared
> to me" (1 Cor. 15:3-8).

The accepted character and claims of Jesus. On numerous occasions Jesus spoke of His crucifixion and resurrection. He claimed He was God (see John 8:58; 10:30; 14:9), and He said He would come back from the dead (see Matt. 16:21). To claim Jesus as a great religious figure and moral teacher while believing that His prediction of His resurrection was wrong would make Him either a liar or a lunatic. The resurrection is essential to the confession that Jesus is Lord. Everything hinges on it.

Reliable eyewitness documents recording the events. The New Testament is the most well-authenticated document of antiquity, a fact no textual critic of any theological persuasion would deny. More than 5,300 Greek manuscripts of the New Testament exist. These are of an earlier date and of a more reliable nature than any other work of antiquity. The New Testament books were all written before the end of the first century and have been substantiated by archaeology. Eyewitness followers of Christ wrote many of them, and the books themselves have the ring of history. No religion has in its sacred writings what Christians have in the New Testament.[37]

These arguments form objective, historically verifiable evidence of Jesus' resurrection. Combined with a believer's personal experience of Jesus as living Lord, they provide ample reason to believe that Jesus was physically raised from the dead by the mighty hand of God.

The Relevance of Jesus' Resurrection

Read the following Scripture references. Record the doctrine(s) that Christ's resurrection verifies, according to each Scripture or group of Scriptures.

Scripture	Doctrine(s)
Acts 2:22-24; Romans 1:3-4	_____
Acts 17:30	_____
Acts 17:31	_____
1 Corinthians 6:14	_____
1 Peter 1:3-5	_____

"It is Jesus of Nazareth who anchors us within that eternal life by giving us his own Spirit and life. … To die in Christ is to have one's entire life upheld by the life of the one who was born, who died, and who continues to live beyond the power of death."[36]
—*John P. Newport*

The resurrection has theological significance for Christian belief and practice today. It verifies the truthfulness of doctrines like the deity of Jesus Christ (see Acts 2:22-24; Rom. 1:3-4), the gospel itself (see Acts 17:30), the reality of heaven (see 1 Pet. 1:3-5), and hope for the believer's resurrection (see Rom. 6:8-9; 1 Cor. 6:14; 15:20-28; 2 Cor. 4:14; 5:10; Phil. 3:21; 1 Thess. 4:14; 1 John 3:2). The resurrection indicates God's approval of Jesus—who He is and what He said. God's approval includes Jesus' message about the way people can receive eternal life (see John 14:6). The resurrection is unlike any other miracle, for its very occurrence involves eternal life. Jesus' resurrection was the very manifestation of eternal life. He was raised in a physical body that was transformed. Jesus is now immortal; He will never die again. When the disciples witnessed Jesus' resurrection appearances, they were actually confronted with living, walking, and talking eternal life. Jesus' resurrection confirms that this existence is a reality for all of His followers.[38]

First Corinthians 15, in particular, emphasizes the importance and nature of Christ's resurrection and its significance for believers. The validity of the Christian faith rests on it (see vv. 12-19). It is integral to the gospel (see vv. 1-11), our future hope (see vv. 20-28), and Christian ethics (see vv. 29-34). Because a believer's salvation, motivation, and anticipation are based on the resurrection, this doctrine should have a significant priority in every ministry. It is the foundation of steadfastness and fruitfulness in the work of the Lord, because laborers can be assured that their labor is not in vain (see v. 58).

The resurrection is at the core of the Christian gospel and Christian theology. It tells us that the God who raised Jesus from the dead exists. It establishes Jesus' lordship. It establishes the doctrine of justification, which was accomplished on the cross and vindicated by Jesus' resurrection. The resurrection promises victory over death (see John 14:1-9; 1 Cor. 15:55-57), and it is a pledge of God's final judgment (see Acts 17:31; Heb. 9:26-27).

In our postmodern world some might ask, "So what if Jesus rose from the dead? I'm glad it works for you, but it's not for me." How should we respond to those who may not deny Jesus' bodily resurrection but who question its significance and relevance for them today?

Several years ago I participated in a short-term mission trip to Thailand. Almost totally Buddhist, this country is very resistant to Christianity. One day we hired a guide to take us around Bangkok to see the sights. As we began talking, I told him that I was a Christian. He politely informed me that he was a Buddhist, and then he asked me to explain what a Christian is. To my shame and amazement he told me that he had never heard about Jesus. He kindly allowed me to talk for some time, and when I told him about Jesus' crucifixion and resurrection, he literally stopped the car and

" '[God] has set a day on which He is going to judge the world in righteousness by the Man He has appointed. He has provided proof of this to everyone by raising Him from the dead' " (Acts 17:31).

"With confidence we understand that the dead in Christ shall rise. With anticipation we await the day when the saints will reign with him, and our vision is of the Lamb who shall rule from His throne."[39]
—*R. Albert Mohler, Jr.*

turned to me in the backseat to ask if I had really said that Jesus was raised from the dead. I said that was correct, and I went on to tell him that Jesus remains alive today as God and King over all things. When I finished, the Buddhist said nothing for several minutes. He then looked at me and said, "If this Jesus really did come back to life from the dead, He did something that no one else has ever done. If that is true, He would have the right to make a claim on every person that no one else could."

This Buddhist man did not become a Christian that day. He said he could not believe that someone could come back from the dead, but he would think about it. However, the man saw the issue and what is at stake with crystal clarity. This chapter shows that Jesus is indeed the risen Lord. You can reject Him, but you cannot ignore Him. What Jesus did in rising from the dead demands a response. How will you respond to the risen Lord and King of the universe? It is a question that cannot be avoided.

Your non-Christian neighbor has come over with questions for you. Respond to each one, using extra paper if needed.

"The claim that Jesus Christ was resurrected from the dead is unbelievable. Everyone knows that dead people don't come back to life! What facts can you give to prove that He was resurrected?"

"But perhaps all the 'facts' you have given me are just legends or myths. I have read that even some Christian scholars discount the resurrection as just a story with no historical truth. How do you respond to that?"

"If Jesus is alive, what difference does He make? How has He changed your life?"

"Because he lives we can face the future without fear."[40]
— *Hank Hanegraaff*

117

"Crown Him with
    many crowns,
The Lamb upon
    His throne;
Hark! how the heaven'ly
    anthem drowns
All music but its own:
Awake, my soul, and sing
Of Him who died for thee,
And hail Him as thy
    matchless King
Thro' all eternity.

Crown Him the Lord
    of life,
Who triumphed
    o'er the grave,
And rose victorious
    in the strife
For those He came to save;
His glories now we sing
Who died, and rose
    on high,
Who died eternal life
    to bring,
And lives that death
    may die."[41]

"When you have hard times and face problems and adversity, how does Jesus help you?"

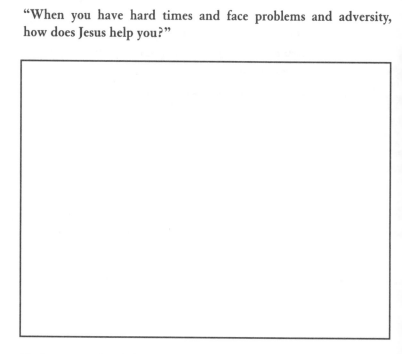

End your study of this chapter by singing the song in the margin as an affirmation of your faith in and commitment to Christ, your resurrected Savior and Lord.

Answers to activity on page 114: Acts 2:22-24; Romans 1:3-4: Christ (lordship, deity, Sonship), God (omniscience, omnipotence), Holy Spirit. Acts 17:30: salvation. Acts 17:31: Christ, Last Things (judgment). 1 Corinthians 6:14: God (omnipotence), Last Things (believers' resurrection). 1 Peter 1:3-5: salvation (new birth, hope, eternal security), God (omnipotence), Last Things (heaven).

Chapter 6
Who Do You Say I Am?

Several years ago I attended a worship service that targeted Generation X and younger. The leader, Ben Young, was preaching a series on systematic theology, and more than one thousand young people attended each week to learn Bible doctrine. I had been told that young people would not listen to doctrine. That was clearly incorrect.

On this particular night they were discussing Christology. Ben gave a brief but accurate exposition of Colossians 1:15-20, pointing out that—
• when you see Jesus, you see God;
• Jesus, as the divine Son of God, created all things;
• because Jesus is God, He has the right to have first place in your life.
Then he said, "This is what the Bible teaches. Now what has the church believed about who Jesus is?" He told us to open our bulletins. I was amazed to find printed the Nicene Creed of A.D. 325. Ben recounted what led to the formulation of this great Christological statement that affirms Jesus' full deity and perfect humanity.

Then Ben asked the congregation to stand to its feet and, as an act of worship and confession, to recite in unison this ancient creed. When we finished, people clapped, shouted, and cheered. He then gave a gospel invitation, and a number of persons came forward confessing Christ as Savior and Lord.

I left the service stunned at what I had seen. I had never heard the Nicene Creed read or printed in a Baptist church service. How ironic that my first time would be in a gymnasium with young adults and teens in T-shirts, shorts, and sandals!

What does the Bible say about Jesus? What has the church believed about Jesus? What is your confession about Christ? Those three questions represent the major responses we can make to Jesus. We have already examined what the Bible teaches about the person and work of Christ. In this final chapter we will survey the historical record of the church's beliefs about Jesus, and we will discover what some churches are teaching today. We will then conclude our study on a personal level: What should be our response to the Jesus who is revealed in the Bible? What are some guiding principles for someone who is committed to living daily under the lordship of Jesus Christ?

Chapter 6 Learning Goals
• You will understand erroneous views about Jesus at the time of the early church and today.
• You will be able to summarize the historical positions of the church on the person and work of Jesus.
• You will be able to share your faith with others and recommit to live under the lordship of Christ.
Ask God to speak to your heart as you study.

The Witness of History to Jesus of Nazareth

The church has always believed certain basic tenets about the person and work of Jesus Christ.

1. The second person of the triune God was truly incarnated. The Son of God actually took on the whole of human nature.
2. Jesus Christ was one person who possessed the totality of both the divine and human natures.
3. The result of the incarnation was the God-man Jesus Christ. He was not a double being, a compound being, or a hybrid being. Our Lord Jesus Christ was one person, complete in His deity and perfect in His humanity.
4. Neither Christ's deity nor His humanity was compromised or diminished in the incarnation. Each nature retained its own integrity and genuineness.
5. The divine nature and the human nature came together in the one person Jesus Christ. This union was real, supernatural, personal, inseparable, and permanent. Jesus is still the God-man who is in heaven "at the right hand of the Majesty on high" (Heb. 1:3) and "always lives to intercede for [us]" (Heb. 7:25).
6. The whole of Christ's work—all He does and has done—must be attributed to His person and not exclusively to either His divine or human nature.
7. Jesus of Nazareth came to be only by means of the incarnation. There was a time when Jesus of Nazareth did not exist, but there has never been a time when God the Son did not exist.[2]

The Apostles' Creed dates from the fifth to seventh centuries, but parts date back to about A.D. 100. Read the creed in the margin slowly and carefully. Then read it again, this time aloud. Finally, write the part of the creed that affirms each of the following.

Jesus' deity: _____

Jesus' virgin birth: _____

Jesus' humanity: _____

Jesus' death: _____

Jesus' resurrection: _____

The Apostles' Creed
"I believe in God, the
   Father almighty,
creator of heaven and earth.
I believe in Jesus Christ,
   God's only Son, our Lord,
He was conceived by
   the Holy Spirit
and born of the Virgin Mary,
He suffered under Pontius
   Pilate,
was crucified, died,
   and was buried.
He descended to the dead.
On the third day he rose
   again.
He ascended into heaven,
and is seated at the right
   hand of the Father.
He will come again
   to judge the living
   and the dead."[1]

Jesus' present position: _____

Jesus' return to earth: _____

During the first five hundred years of church history the church actively wrestled with how to understand and comprehend the biblical portrait of Jesus. Two issues in particular guided the conversation: the monotheism (belief in one God) that Christianity inherited from Judaism and the fact that the New Testament clearly affirmed Jesus as God. How could these competing truths be reconciled?

The Rise of Heresies

The development of a number of heretical teachings forced the church to confront the issue of Christ's deity and its monotheistic faith early in its history.

Docetism. John wrote his first letter, in part, to confront a heresy known as docetism, which he encountered in and around Ephesus. Docetism comes from the Greek word *dokeo,* which means *to seem* or *appear.* Denying the reality of Jesus' body, as well as His sufferings and death, docetists claimed that Jesus only appeared to have a body. These false teachers refused to confess Jesus as the Christ (see 1 John 2:22) and denied that the Son had come in the flesh (see 1 John 4:2-3; 2 John 7).

The Church Father Ignatius (died c. A.D. 110) countered docetism in his letter to the Ephesians: "There is only one physician, who is both flesh and spirit, born and unborn, God in man, true life in death, both from Mary and from God, first subject to suffering and then beyond it, Jesus Christ our Lord."[3] Again in his letter to the Trallians Ignatius charged: "Be deaf, therefore, whenever anyone speaks to you apart from Jesus Christ, who was of the family of David, who was the son of Mary; who really was born, who both ate and drank; who really was persecuted under Pontius Pilate, who really was crucified and died … who, moreover, really was raised from the dead. … But if, as some atheists (that is, unbelievers) say, he suffered in appearance only (while they exist in appearance only!), why am I in chains? And why do I want to fight with wild beasts? If that is the case, I die for no reason; what is more, I am telling lies about the Lord."[4]

Gnosticism. Docetists were likely influenced by early gnostic ideas that flourished in the second century. We might call gnosticism the New Age Movement of that day. The word *gnosis* in Greek means *knowledge.* Though gnosticism developed into many forms, two basic teachings were always present: (1) salvation comes by way of mystical knowledge, and (2) matter is inferior or evil. Gnosticism teaches that a great distance separates God

> "Who is the liar, if not the one who denies that Jesus is the Messiah? He is the antichrist, the one who denies the Father and the Son" (1 John 2:22).

"Jesus Christ—He is the One who came by water and blood; not by water only, but by water and by blood. And the Spirit is the One who testifies, because the Spirit is the truth. For there are three that testify: the Spirit, the water, and the blood—and these three are in agreement" (1 John 5:6-8).

and the material world. Spirit and matter exist but seriously oppose each other. The human spirit/soul is alienated and separated from God and is trapped in an evil body.

God, who had nothing to do with the creation of the material world, sent Christ to rescue our souls. This Christ could not have been incarnate, however, for this would have involved His taking to Himself sinful and evil flesh. Therefore, Christ only appeared to have a body, as claimed by docetism, an argument John refuted in John 1:1,14,18 and 1 John 1:1-4, or Christ temporarily adopted the man Jesus, as taught by a man named Cerinthius. In this view Christ came upon the man Jesus at His baptism (see Matt. 3:13-17) but left Him prior to His death on the cross (see Matt. 27:46). John refuted this heresy in 1 John 5:6-8.[5]

The Church Father Irenaeus (c. 130–200) exposed the error of the gnostics, including the teachings of Cerinthius: "John, the disciple of the Lord, proclaimed this faith and wished by the proclamation of the gospel to destroy the error which had been planted among men by Cerinthius. ... Now according to them neither was the Word made flesh, nor Christ, nor the Savior. ... For they allege that the Word and Christ never came into this world, and that the Savior was neither incarnate nor suffered, but that he descended as a dove upon that Jesus ... and when he had proclaimed the unknown Father, ascended again."[6]

Ebionism. Ebionism was another early heresy that rejected the reality of the incarnation and the deity of Jesus. Ebionites claimed that Jesus was the prophet whom Moses predicted in Deuteronomy 18:15, but He was not the preexistent Son of God. Holding a form of adoptionism similar to the teaching of Cerinthius, ebionites taught that Jesus was made the Anointed One at His baptism, and He was chosen because of His perfect obedience to the law, which they esteemed highly.[7] Irenaeus also addressed this teaching: "Vain also are the Ebionites who do not accept in their souls by faith the union of God and man ... not wishing to understand that the Holy Spirit came upon Mary, and the power of the Most High overshadowed her, and so what was born [of her] is holy and the Son of God Most High."[8]

Essential subordination. Debate and discussion about the person of Christ, His nature, and His relationship to the Father would continue into the second and third centuries. Origen (c. 185–254) argued that the Son had existed from eternity but also that the Son was subordinate to the Father in His essence, being, and person.[9]

Adoptionism. Others, like Theodotus of Byzantium and Paul of Samosata (c. 260), argued that God adopted Jesus as a unique and special man on whom His power would rest. Again, these teachings denied Jesus' full deity and eternality. This heresy would be modified by men named Lucian and Arius, and it would provide the catalyst for the Nicene Council.

Modalism. Some wanted to maintain monotheism while affirming Jesus' deity. The false teaching of modalism claimed that the three persons of the deity are simply three ways or modes in which the one God revealed or manifested Himself. Father, Son, and Holy Spirit are in a sense simply names that apply to the same person. It could be said that the Father was born in Bethlehem and was crucified at Calvary, but at the time He was manifest as the Son and was called Jesus.

In refuting this heresy, the Church Father Tertullian (c. 155–220) made an important contribution to the doctrines of theology proper (God) and Christology by introducing the terms *Trinity, unity of substance,* and *three Persons* into the discussion of the relationship among Father, Son, and Holy Spirit. He wrote that modalism "supposes itself to possess the pure truth, in thinking that one cannot believe in One Only God in any other way than by saying that the Father, the Son, and the Holy Ghost are the very selfsame Person. As if in this way also one were not All, in that All are of One, by unity (that is) of substance …, which distributes the Unity into a Trinity, placing in their order the three Persons—the Father, the Son, and the Holy Ghost."[10] However, Tertullian did not work out the implications of these terms. That would come about in the first four Councils of the church: Nicea in 325, Constantinople in 381, Ephesus in 431, and Chalcedon in 451.

"Jesus Christ is the same yesterday, today, and forever" (Heb. 13:8).

Match each heretical belief about Christ with its description.

___ 1. Adoptionism   ___ 4. Docetism

___ 2. Ebionism   ___ 5. Essential subordination

___ 3. Modalism   ___ 6. Gnosticism

a. God revealed Himself in three different ways: the Father became Jesus who, when He died, became the Holy Spirit.

b. The Son had existed from eternity but was subordinate to the Father in essence, being, and person.

c. Jesus only appeared to have a body.

d. God took Jesus as a unique and special man on whom His power would rest.

e. Christ came upon Jesus at His baptism but left Him prior to His death on the cross.

f. Jesus was a prophet predicted by Moses, but He was not the eternal, preexistent Son of God.

Read again the Apostles' Creed on page 120. How does it refute the following heretical teachings?

The Nicene Creed
"We believe in one God the Father Almighty, Maker of all things visible and invisible; and in one Lord Jesus Christ, the only begotten of the Father, that is, of the substance [*ousias*] of the Father, God of God, light of light, true God of true God, begotten not made, of the same substance with the Father [*homoousion*], through whom all things were made both in heaven and on earth; who for us men and our salvation descended, was incarnate, and was made man, suffered and rose again the third day, ascended into heaven and cometh to judge the living and the dead. And in the Holy Ghost. Those who say: There was a time when He was not, and He was not before He was begotten; and that He was made out of nothing; or who maintain that He is of another hypostasis or another substance [than the Father], or that the Son of God is created, or mutable, or subject to change, [them] the Catholic Church anathematizes."[11]

A denial of Jesus' humanity: _____

A denial of Jesus' deity: _____

The Council of Nicea

The Roman emperor Constantine, who had allegedly experienced a conversion to Christianity, gave safety and political clout to the Christian movement as he gained power in the Roman Empire. His goal was to keep the empire unified, but a major theological dispute between Alexander, Bishop of Alexandria (died 328), and one of his presbyters, Arius (c. 250–336), put a significant obstacle in the way. Arius had adopted the heresy of Paul of Samosata, which taught that Jesus had become Godlike when the Holy Spirit came upon Him at His baptism. This teaching emphasized Jesus' manhood but undermined His deity. When Paul of Samosata thought of the Word being in Jesus, it meant only the impersonal power of God. Jesus, then, was a mere man who was controlled by the power of God.

Arius also viewed Jesus as less than fully God. Considering that only one true God exists who is eternal, immutable, and indivisible, Arius concluded that Christ must be of a different substance. God must have created Christ. And if Christ was created, His essence was substantially different from God's; yet He was created from nothing. Thus, the Arian party held two main points of contention at the time of the Council of Nicea: Jesus was not coeternal, and He was created from nothing.

Arius was opposed by Alexander and his young protégé, Athanasius (c. 296–373). Constantine brought together the leaders of the church in A.D. 325, and supporters of both Arius and Alexander were present among approximately 318 bishops who attended. Debate centered on the key term *homoousion,* which affirmed that the Son was fully divine and of the same substance or essence as the Father. Alexander and his followers were successful, and the result of the first Church Council is what we know as the Nicene Creed. Stop and read it in the margin.

Circle each part of the creed that deals with Jesus' deity, humanity, death, resurrection, ascension, and return.

Underline phrases in the creed that are difficult for you to understand. Admittedly, it is a heavy theological document.

The Nicene Council was crucial in establishing what the church believed the Bible taught about the person of Christ. Craig Blaising summarizes what the Nicene Creed accomplished: "The theology expressed in the Nicene Creed is decisively anti-Arian. At the beginning the unity of God is affirmed. But the Son is said to be 'true God from true God.' ... It is positively asserted that he is 'from the being (*ousias*) of the Father' and 'of one substance (*homoousion*) with the Father.' A list of Arian phrases, including 'there was when he was not' and assertions that the Son is a creature or out of nothing, are expressly anathematized [denounced]. Thus, an ontological [essential or real] rather than merely functional deity of the Son was upheld at Nicea."[12]

The Council of Constantinople

Called by Emperor Theodosius in 381, this council put an end to Arianism, which had experienced several resurgences in the 50 years following Nicea. The Council of Contantinople essentially reaffirmed the decision of the Council of Nicea and completed the final version of the Nicene Creed. It also condemned the teachings of a man named Appollinarius (c. 310–90).

If Arius erred by denying the deity of the Son, Appollinarius erred by overemphasizing it. Appollinarius was a staunch defender of the Nicene doctrine and a former friend of Athanasius. He taught that while all other human beings are body, soul, and spirit coexisting in a union, Christ had only the human body and soul, the divine *Logos* having displaced the human spirit. Christ was perfect God, but He lacked a complete humanity. Appollinarius interpreted John 1:14 very literally: Jesus took on a human body alone, not the human spirit. Jesus, then, did not have a human will, only a divine will. Hence, Jesus had a human body and a divine spirit.

This view denies Jesus' full humanity. Not only our human bodies but also our souls and spirits need redemption. Christ had to be fully and truly man to save our entire selves. As Gregory of Nazianzus argued, "That which he has not assumed He has not healed; but that which is united to his Godhead is also saved."[13] Constantinople affirmed the full humanity of God's Son.

The Council of Ephesus

In 431 this council condemned a man named Nestorius, who purportedly believed that two separate persons resided in Christ, a human person and a divine person. Nowhere in Scripture does Christ's human nature act as an independent person, deciding to do something contrary to His divine nature. Rather, Jesus consistently acted in wholeness and unity. Rejecting Nestorianism, the council insisted that Jesus was one person who possessed both a human nature and a divine nature.

> "There are people who have emphasized Christ's deity over His humanity, to the point that some forget that He was human. There are others who are emphasizing His humanity and deny His deity. He was both— God and man. He was: 'The God-man.' "[14]
> —*Billy Graham*

The Council of Chalcedon

This is the final and climactic of the four great Christological councils. Incorporating the major components of the three previous councils, it solidified and established what the church believes the Bible teaches about the person of Christ.

The council also condemned, excommunicated, and deposed a man named Eutyches (c. 378–454), the head of a large monastery in Constantinople, for his teaching. Eutyches believed that Christ's human nature was taken up and absorbed into the divine nature, so that both natures were changed, and thus a new, third kind of nature resulted. Jesus, according to this view, was a mixture of divine and human elements in which both were somewhat modified to form one new nature.

> "Both His humanity and deity are absolutely essential to His mediatorial work."[15]
> —*R. Albert Mohler, Jr.*

This view presents Jesus as neither truly God nor truly man. Therefore, He could not truly represent us as a human being, nor could He be true God and thus be qualified to pay our sin penalty and redeem us as our substitute. In 451, 630 bishops gathered at the summons of the Eastern Emperor Marcion and formulated a doctrinal statement. This creed sought to summarize and address every problem that had plagued the church about the person of Christ. It argued against the false teachings in the following ways.

1. It rejected docetism by stating that the Lord Jesus was perfect in His humanity and truly human, born of the virgin Mary.
2. It rejected adoptionism by arguing for the eternality of the *Logos* "begotten of the Father before the ages." Christ has always existed as the Son.
3. It rejected modalism by distinguishing the Son from the Father. The creed made this distinction both by using the titles of Father and Son and by stating that the Father had begotten the Son before time began. The Father is not the Son.
4. It rejected Arianism by affirming that the Lord Jesus was perfect in His deity—truly God.
5. It rejected Appollinarianism by confessing that the Lord Jesus Christ was "truly man of a reasonable soul [spirit] and body ... consubstantial [of the same substance] with us according to his humanity; in all things like unto us."
6. It rejected Nestorianism by affirming Jesus' full deity and real incarnation. Throughout it also spoke of one and the same Son, one person and one being, not parted or divided into two persons, whose natures are in union without division and without separation.
7. It rejected Eutychianism by confessing that Christ possessed two natures without confusion and without change, the property of each nature being preserved and existing together in the one person.

Chalcedon argued that Christ is "one person with two natures," the person being that of the Son of the triune God. The eternal Son of God took to himself a truly human nature, and Christ's divine and human natures remain distinct and retain their own properties. Yet they are eternally and inseparably united together in one person. In other words, Jesus Christ is fully God and fully man. Taking on a human nature did not involve mixing divine and human attributes or converting one nature to the other. The two natures are inseparably joined together in one person now and forever.

Nicene-Chalcedonian Christology affirms that in our Lord Jesus Christ we come face-to-face with God. We meet God not subsumed under human flesh, not merely associated with it, not merely accompanying it, and not merely shining through it but in undiminished moral splendor, giving to humanity the moral completeness that has been missing since the time of the fall. The divine Word, then, was not united to a human nature that was foreign to His own life; rather, the divine Word already possessed everything that was necessary to be human. The deity and humanity coincide, not because the human has grown into the divine but because the divine has taken the human into itself in an action in which the human reaches its fulfillment. In Christ we see all that Adam was intended to be but never was, all that we are not but will become through resurrection and glorification (see 1 John 3:1-3).[16]

> **"When He appears, we will be like Him, because we will see Him as He is"** (1 John 3:2).

Christology in the Church Councils

Error Against Deity	Error Against Humanity	Church Position
Arius: Christ was a created being.		Nicea: Affirmed that Christ is eternal and truly God.
	Appollinarius: The divine *Logos* displaced the human spirit.	Constantinople: Affirmed Christ's full humanity.
Nestorius: Two separate persons resided in Christ.		Ephesus: Affirmed unity of Christ's personality.
	Eutyches: Christ's human nature was absorbed by the divine nature.	Chalcedon: Established orthodox Christology: two natures in one person.

Modern Attacks on the Biblical Jesus

As we move into the 21st century, the Jesus question is a hot item of debate. The Christ found in the Bible and confessed by the church for most of its history is no longer acceptable to some people. Attacks come from several directions; yet virtually every attack is composed of two common characteristics:
1. Denial of Christ's deity
2. Rejection of Christ's work on the cross as the sufficient provision for salvation

I want to highlight a couple of the more prominent opponents to biblical and historical Christology.

The Jesus of Liberal Theologians

Friedrich Schleiermacher (1768–1834), the father of modern liberal theology, helped launch the attacks on the Jesus of the Bible. Schleiermacher offered an adoptionist understanding of Jesus that rejected His preexistence. Jesus was not the eternal Son of God who became human, the *Logos* incarnate. For Schleiermacher, what distinguished Jesus from other humans was "the constant potency of his God-consciousness, which was a veritable existence of God in him."[18] Recommending belief in inspiration instead of incarnation, he presented Jesus as a God-filled man, not the God-man. This Jesus, who differed from us only in having been a better person than we are, is an inspiring example for us to follow. But He is not our Savior in the biblical understanding.

Between 1880 and 1920 the history-of-religions school argued that Christ's preexistence and incarnation are only myths intended to give Him a stature equal to that of other heroic figures of His day. The doctrine of Jesus' preexistence resulted from the attempt to push His divine status earlier and earlier in His existence. These scholars distinguished between the Jesus of history—the man who actually lived—and the Christ of faith—the mythical Christ created in the mind of the early church.

From this boiling cauldron emerged the quest for the historical Jesus. With post-Enlightenment skepticism, antisupernatural bias, and rigorous scientific methodology, this quest began in earnest in the latter part of the 19th century and continues today. We can identify three phases of the modern quest.

The first quest. The Life of Jesus, written by David Friedrich Strauss in 1835–36, shook the theological world by questioning the Gospel accounts as accurate historical records of Jesus' words and deeds. The first quest for the historical Jesus—the Jesus behind what were claimed to be embellished Gospels—was off and running. The search moved forward until Albert Schweitzer halted its progress with his landmark work *The Quest for the*

> "All else is secondary to the question of what one thinks of Christ."[17]
> —*Millard J. Erickson*

Historical Jesus in 1906. Schweitzer, himself a liberal, demonstrated that these scholars ignored the significant dimensions of Jesus' life, teachings, and actions and that their Jesus looked suspiciously like them!

The second quest. A new quest for the historical Jesus began around 1950. In 1953 Ernst Käsemann suggested that even though the Gospel traditions reflected the perspectives of Jesus' followers, they could not be completely discounted as witnesses of authentic historical evidence. The second, so-called New Quest was inaugurated. The Jesus of the New Questers was also distorted, looking suspiciously like an existentialist philosopher. This is not surprising because that worldview greatly influenced the presuppositions of the New Quest's most influential scholars. Existentialism emphasizes an individual's experience and responsibility in a world that is viewed as meaningless and without a moral compass to guide right and wrong. The New Quest experienced a setback in the early 1970s when existentialism waned.

The third quest. A period of reevaluation, methodological refinement, and new archaeological and manuscript evidence created a renewed sense that historians could find the historical Jesus, the Jesus behind the Gospels. Since the 1980s the number of scholars who have written major works on the historical Jesus has exploded. Entering through door number 1 are those looking for a Jewish Jesus in a first-century context. They argue that the Gospels contain reliable material that tells us what Jesus did and taught. Entering through door number 2 is the infamous Jesus Seminar, which is essentially an extension of the New Questers. The Jesus Seminar argues that the biblical portrait of Jesus is mostly a theological creation of the early church.

The third quest has offered multiple, competing portraits of Jesus, portraits that picture Him as a first-century Jew, a revolutionary, a cynic-like sage, a reforming teacher of Judaism, a prophet, a restorer/reformer of Israel, and/or a messianic claimant.[19]

> "The Word became flesh and took up residence among us. We observed His glory, the glory as the One and Only Son from the Father, full of grace and truth" (John 1:14).

The Jesus Seminar

The Jesus Seminar appeared in the mid-1980s and emerged full-fledged with its publication of *The Five Gospels* in 1993. The Seminar convened to determine what Jesus actually said. It rated each saying in Matthew, Mark, Luke, John, and the nonbiblical Gospel of Thomas according to a color code. Red means Jesus said exactly what the Gospels recorded. Pink indicates He said something very close to what was recorded. Grey means the words were that of the evangelist, but they have roots in Jesus' teaching. Black means the sayings have no connection to Jesus at all; they simply reflected the theological interest of the early church.[20]

Only 18 percent of the sayings received a red or pink rating. Approximately 50 percent were rated black. The Seminar argued that 82 percent of the words attributed to Jesus do not come from Him. Jesus, it argues, was not interested in eschatology or judgment. He was basically a teacher who used humorous sayings and parables. The Seminar concluded that much of what we find in the Gospels is the early church's work and does not originate with Jesus.

Evangelical Christians must recognize that the Jesus Seminar's method and conclusions have serious shortcomings.

1. Its antisupernatural worldview biased its evaluation of the biblical material. It was not open to where the data might lead because it had determined in advance where it must lead: to a purely human Jesus who cannot be God.
2. The group ignored the fact that all the information we have on Jesus demands that He look like a first-century Jew who spent His life in Israel.
3. The object of Christian faith is the triune God revealed in history and the Old and New Testaments. In the Old Testament we discover the promise of a Savior, and in the New Testament we witness the coming of that Savior. The questers failed to appreciate the flow of redemptive history.
4. The Jesus of history and the Christ of faith cannot be separated, for they are one and the same. Each quest, including the Jesus Seminar, has failed at some point by separating them.
5. All evidence indicates that the church's high Christology has its source in Jesus and that worship of Jesus as God was practiced from the beginning. Stephen Davis puts it this way:

> A convincing case can be made that much of the material in the Gospels that implies a high Christology can in some form be traced back to Jesus, and that he implicitly claimed the high status that the church attributed to him. Here is one telling fact about the earliest Christians: They practiced worship of Jesus. Early Christian prayers were addressed to Jesus, one preserved even in Aramaic ("Maranatha"), which attests to its earliness (1 Cor. 16:22; see also 2 Cor. 12:8; 1 Thess. 3:11-13; 2 Thess. 2:16-17; 3:5,16; Acts 1:24; 7:59-60). There were also doxologies addressed to Christ, or to Christ and the Father together (Rom. 16:27; cf. 2 Cor. 1:20; 2 Tim. 4:18; 2 Peter 3:18; Rev. 1:5-6, 13; cf. 7:10), and hymns of praise to Christ (Phil. 2:6-11; 1 Tim. 3:16; cf. Eph. 5:19; Col. 3:16). In Matthew's Gospel, after the resurrection, Jesus is worshiped (*proskynesis*) by Mary Magdalene and the other Mary (28:9) and by the 11 disciples on the mountain (28:17).[21]

"May our Lord Jesus Christ Himself and God our Father, who has loved us and given us eternal encouragement and good hope by grace, encourage your hearts and strengthen you in every good work and word" (2 Thess. 2:16-17).

6. If Jesus was little more than a witty sage or a cynical philosopher who spoke only in short, pithy sayings and parables, why was He crucified? What threat was He to either the Jewish authorities or the Roman government? Such a Jesus would have challenged certain social and cultural conventions in His day, but this is hardly the kind of activity that gets someone nailed to a cross.

7. The work of the Jesus Seminar, in particular, was not really new. It was simply a continuation of the antisupernatural approach of persons like Rudolf Bultmann who attempted (and failed) to get back to the historical Jesus by stripping away anything that looked supernatural and seeing what was left. The result was a Jesus who could not have inspired worship, much less martyrdom, on the part of His followers.

8. The uncertainties of critical scholars and the varied portraits they paint of Jesus should make us skeptical of their conclusions. If they are fair and objective with the evidence, why can't they agree on who Jesus was? Do their biases, prejudices, and agendas lead them to discover a Jesus they like, a Jesus who is merely a voice for their own ideologies?[22]

9. The Gospels were written from the standpoint of faith for the purpose of spreading the faith. The biblical texts themselves honestly admit this fact. Their original purpose does not lessen their credibility but actually enhances it. James Edwards says, "Modern scholarship has correctly shown that the Gospels are not strict biographies, but presentations of Jesus told from the standpoint of faith and for the purpose of furthering faith. The Gospels are part of the *kerygma,* the proclamation of the early church, which means that Jesus can be known only through the testimony of his followers. Liberal scholarship errs, however, in assuming that this testimony results in a distortion of the historical Jesus."[23]

10. Numerous eyewitnesses were alive when the Gospels were written. They certainly would have functioned as custodians and protectors of the testimony about Jesus.

Though additional evidence could be brought to this study to defend the reliability of the Jesus we find in the Bible, we will end this section with this: "The most reasonable answer to the question why the Gospels present Jesus as they do is because that is essentially who Jesus was. The Gospels faithfully preserve the memory that He left on His followers, that He was divinely legitimated and empowered to be God's Son and Servant."[24] This is the Jesus of Scripture. This is the Jesus confessed by the believing church. And this is the Jesus we worship and serve as Lord. Let's explore what it means to live under the lordship of Jesus Christ.

> " 'You don't have His word living in you, because you don't believe the One He sent. You pore over the Scriptures because you think you have eternal life in them, yet they testify about Me. And you are not willing to come to Me that you may have life' " (John 5:38-40).

131

Living Under the Lordship of Jesus Christ

Because of who Jesus is and what He has done, believers are called to live daily under His lordship. Paul challenged the Colossians in this regard when he wrote: "Whatever you do, do it enthusiastically [do it from the soul], as something done for the Lord and not for men, knowing that you will receive the reward of an inheritance from the Lord—you serve the Lord Christ" (Col. 3:23-24).

Paul also urged those in Rome "to present your bodies as a living sacrifice, holy and pleasing to God" (Rom. 12:1). He grounded this challenge in "the mercies of God," a reference to Romans 1—11, and in particular the work of Christ, which is addressed in Romans 3:21—8:39. In 1 Corinthians Paul added, "Do you not know that your body is a sanctuary of the Holy Spirit who is in you, whom you have from God? You are not your own, for you were bought at a price; therefore glorify God in your body" (1 Cor. 6:19-20). The great Bible teacher W. H. Griffith Thomas captured what Paul said by writing, "Every part of our life is to be His."[25]

Scripture connects the person and work of Christ to the believer's sanctification, the process of growing in Christlikeness. Living under Christ's lordship makes a difference in our lives, and the Bible provides principles and guidelines for honoring Christ.

First Corinthians is an excellent place to begin. The Corinthians had been saved, some from lifestyles of sexual immorality, idolatry, adultery, male prostitution, homosexuality, thievery, greed, drunkenness, slandering, and dishonesty (see 1 Cor. 6:9-10). By the atoning work of Christ, Paul could now say that they "were washed, ... sanctified, ... justified in the name of the Lord Jesus Christ and by the Spirit of our God" (1 Cor. 6:11). However, they still faced the daily struggles and challenges of practicing their new life in Christ. Paul helped them and us by providing basic, wise principles that guide us to be good decision makers and live under the lordship of Christ. We can apply Paul's wise counsel to every decision we face.

Principle 1: Will this action edify me (see 1 Cor. 6:12)? A group in the church at Corinth had adopted some bad theology. Similar in some ways to the gnostics, they held "a false view of freedom ('everything is permissible') and of the body ('God will destroy it'), from which basis they argued that going to prostitutes is permissible because the body doesn't matter."[26] Thus, the phrase " 'Everything is permissible for me,' " found twice in verse 12 (also see 1 Cor. 10:23), was almost certainly a boast of the theologically confused at Corinth.[27]

" 'Everything is permissible for me,' but not everything is helpful. 'Everything is permissible for me,' but I will not be brought under the control of anything" (1 Cor. 6:12).

Paul counterpunched by saying, "But not everything is helpful." Not every action builds us up, profits us, or helps us personally. Not every action enables us to live under the lordship of Jesus Christ. Although the context of Paul's words is probably sexual immorality, it would be a mistake to limit the application of this principle to that alone. What we think about, look at, and listen to; what we take into our bodies and do with our bodies; how we spend our time—are we living in ways that will edify us, build us up, and help us personally? Paul said to ask this question before we act.

Principle 2: Will this action enslave me (see 1 Cor. 6:12)?

> Read 1 Corinthians 6:12 from several translations. Then write your paraphrase of this verse.

_____

_____

Paul challenged the second " 'Everything is permissible for me' " boast with a defiant no! "I will not be brought under the control of anything." The word *control* carries the idea of mastered, enslaved, or overpowered.[28] Nothing and nobody would have mastery over Paul but Jesus. If a particular activity has the potential to enslave us emotionally, physically, psychologically, or chemically, we must say no to it. John MacArthur puts it well: "Paul was free in the grace of God to do as he pleased, but he refused to allow himself to be mastered by anything or anyone but Christ. He would not become enslaved to any habit or custom and certainly not to any sin."[29]

This principle is especially relevant to the areas of alcohol, drugs, tobacco, and pornography. Because each of these has a great capacity to enslave and overpower, a wise believer will stay as far away as possible from activities that have destroyed countless lives, marriages, and families. Everybody is a slave to someone or something. We may be free to choose our master, but we are not free to be without a master. Only Christ must be our master.

Principle 3: Will this action encourage others (see 1 Cor. 8:13)?

> Read 1 Corinthians 8:13 from several translations. Write one sentence that states the meaning in clear, simple language.

_____

_____

"If food causes my brother to fall, I will never again eat meat, so that I won't cause my brother to fall" (1 Cor. 8:13).

133

In first-century Corinth, eating meat that had been sacrificed to an idol became an important issue of conscience. Weaker believers, who were perhaps also new believers recently saved from the pagan world of Corinth, felt it was wrong to eat such meat. Paul knew that "an idol is nothing in the world" (1 Cor. 8:4), but he also knew that "not everyone has this knowledge" (8:7). In fact, "some have been so used to idolatry up until now, that when they eat food offered to an idol, their conscience, being weak, is defiled" (8:7).

Paul reasoned, therefore, that our liberty must be regulated by the principle of lordship (see 8:12). If any particular action is a potential stumbling block to a brother or a sister in the Lord, love for Christ and love for the person must guide our decision making. Fee says, "Love, that is, care for a brother, determines Christian ethical life, not 'freedom.' "[30]

Principle 4: Will this action evangelize the lost (see 1 Cor. 9:19-23; 10:32-33)? Lost people matter to God. Lost people should matter to us. If lordship and love regulate our liberty with a weaker brother or sister, should they not do the same with respect to the lost? Paul evaluated every action with a crucial question in mind: will my action help or harm my witness for Christ? Jesus said in Mark 10:45, " 'Even the Son of Man did not come to be served, but to serve, and to give His life—a ransom for many.' " And in Luke 19:10 our Lord declared, " 'The Son of Man has come to seek and to save the lost.' " If that is Jesus' mission, it must be our mission, and we must not put anything in the way that would hinder people from coming to Christ.

This principle was so urgent in Paul's mind that he addressed it twice in this section of 1 Corinthians. Read verses 19-23 in the margin.

Paul denied himself personal rights and privileges because he lived "under the law of Christ" (9:21). The souls of lost people and the lordship of Christ mattered most to him. Paul willingly accommodated himself both to Jewish and Gentile cultures and expectations as long as they did not violate his devotion and allegiance to Jesus Christ, the Lord. Making the winning of souls a foundational plank in his ministry and lifestyle, he reiterated his commitment when he added, "Give no offense to the Jews or the Greeks or the church of God, just as I also try to please all people in all things, not seeking my own profit, but the profit of many, that they may be saved" (1 Cor. 10:32-33).

We must be careful not to misunderstand Paul's statement. Paul in no way means he would sin or would compromise his message to win sinners. His point is that the only offense that should keep a sinner from being saved must be the offense of the gospel itself (see 1 Cor. 1:21-24).

Principle 5: Will this action emulate the Lord (see 1 Cor. 11:1)? For Paul the supreme example for all of life is Christ. Jesus set the pattern Paul attempted to follow. Peter said the same thing in 1 Peter 2:21:

"Though I am free and belong to no man, I make myself a slave to everyone, to win as many as possible. To the Jews I became a Jew, to win the Jews. To those under the law I became like one under the law (though I myself am not under the law), so as to win those under the law. To those not having the law I became like one not having the law (though I am not free from God's law but am under Christ's law), so as to win those not having the law. To the weak I became weak, to win the weak. I have become all things to all men so that by all possible means I might save some. I do all this for the sake of the gospel, that I may share in its blessings" (1 Cor. 9:19-23, NIV).

You were called to this,
because Christ also suffered for you,
leaving you an example,
so that you should follow in His steps.

WWJD? is not a modern invention, for Paul said to the Corinthians, "Be imitators of me, as I also am of Christ" (11:1). The logic of Paul's argument is very instructive. Christ is our ultimate example. Leaders in the church, like Paul, are to imitate Christ. We can and should imitate our leaders as they imitate Christ. What a word for leaders in the church today! What a word for parents today! Think of the important ramifications of this principle: What would Paul do? What would my minister do? What would Dad do? What would Mom do?

The issue becomes uncomfortably clear, doesn't it? If my four sons did what Dad does, would it come close to being what Christ would do? Our little ones by age and in the faith need flesh-and-blood models to imitate. They need heroes who live under the lordship of Jesus Christ.

Principle 6: Will this action exalt God (see 1 Cor. 10:31)? First Corinthians 10:31 is one of the greatest verses in the Bible.

Read 1 Corinthians 10:31 from several translations. Write your paraphrase of this verse.

_____

_____

_____

"Whether you eat or drink, or whatever you do, do everything for God's glory" (1 Cor. 10:31).

The Shorter Westminster Catechism expresses the import of this verse: "The chief end of man is to glorify God and enjoy Him forever." Paul said to glorify God in everything, not some things or even most things. The command is all-inclusive. No sphere of our lives is excluded from the command to glorify God. As we saw in 1 Corinthians 6:20, Paul wedded this exhortation to Christ's work in redeeming us: "You were bought at a price; therefore glorify God in your body." MacArthur writes, "His glory is to be our life commitment. It is the purpose of our whole life, which now belongs to the Lord."[31]

WWJD? stands for _____

List several issues and concerns in your community and in our nation that would benefit by asking, What would Jesus do?

_____

_____

Sometimes God teaches us His wonderful truth through children. That is how He brought home the truth of 1 Corinthians 10:31 to me. When my sons were young, the idea of glorifying God in everything you do came up as we were talking. Timothy, my youngest son, who was about six or seven, looked at me and asked, "Daddy, how do you glorify God playing football?" Up to that point my boys considered the objective in football to hit your opponent as hard as you can, knock him flat, and run over him. How does that assignment match 1 Corinthians 10:31?

I asked the boys, "Can you think of a really good football player who is also known as a fine Christian?" In unison all four answered, "Reggie White!" At that time Reggie White was an All-Pro defensive lineman with the Green Bay Packers. White is also an ordained Baptist minister who loves Jesus. I then asked the boys, "Does Reggie White talk about Jesus?" "Yes," they said. "Does Reggie White play hard but clean, always giving 100 percent?" "Yes," they said. "Does Reggie White use bad language?" "No!" they shouted. "Does he drink, take drugs, or do other bad things?" "No!" "Does Reggie White pray and invite others to pray with him at the end of every game?" "Yes, Daddy, he does." "Do you think Reggie White uses football to glorify Jesus?" Again with one voice they said, "Yes, Daddy, he does."

Timothy then added, "I guess we're supposed to glorify God in our schoolwork, too!" He had figured it out: "Do everything for God's glory."

Our Blessed Hope

We come now to the close of our study. We have examined the life and work of Christ, beginning with the many promises in the Old Testament of a coming Savior. We have studied His incarnation, His virgin birth, His sinless life, His crucifixion, His resurrection, and His ascension. But there is more: the Lord Jesus Christ is coming back to earth!

The doctrine of Christ's second coming is one of the most widely taught doctrines in the Bible. The Old Testament gives a prominent place to our Lord's second advent, and His return is mentioned more than three hundred times in the New Testament. Every prophecy and teaching in the Bible about